JAMES MACGREGOR
*Preacher, Theologian and
Defender of the Faith*

Rev. Dr James MacGregor (c1890)

JAMES MACGREGOR

Preacher, Theologian and Defender of the Faith

John W Keddie

Scottish Reformed Heritage Publications

First published March 2016
Revised edition June 2018

ISBN: 978-1-326-23555-0

Publisher:
Scottish Reformed Heritage Publications
19 Newton Park
Kirkhill
Inverness-shire

Printed and bound by Lulu (www.lulu.com).

CONTENTS

A few nights ago I happened to be out in the dark, and, looking eastward, was struck with the awful glory of a great light, emanating from some iron-works that shone into the sky. It struck me that such must be the awful glory of the dawning approach of the Son of God to judgement. And then I remembered how very soon I, and we all, must see Him, in a meeting either the most blissful or the most woeful. A lady recently told me of an aged father on his deathbed, who told his children, that his long life on earth appeared to him now as a short morning. So it is to us all. Our life on earth is but a short twilight: to some it is the morning twilight, swiftly shading into eternal day; to others it is the evening twilight, swiftly shading into eternal night: but to all alike, it is but a short twilight: "Behold I come quickly."

— *JAMES MACGREGOR (1864)*

… let us observe, that the God of the Bible has the whole matter fully in His view. Whenever He gives us a side-look into His mind, what we see is, that the number of the saved shall be countlessly multitudinous, as the sand on the sea shore, the stars in the firmament, the dew of the morning. And He says that, with reference to His "seed" the suffering God-man, who gave His life a ransom for many, shall see of the travail of His soul, and shall be satisfied. Perhaps we too, shall be satisfied, if we have patience with the Eternal. It is good for us now, to believe that all depends upon His will. For the number must indeed be great, if the saved be so many as to satisfy the loving heart of God. And there never shall be one saved sinner in the universe if…the matter be made to depend upon the ungodly heart of men

— *JAMES MACGREGOR (1888)*

Dr Philip Schaff, in his work on the "Creeds of Christendom" says that the distinctive point of Augustinianism, or Calvinism, is "love." It really is not so; and it is undesirable that it should be so represented. For it is a desirable result of the system to lead men on the way to great heroic human character, in adoration of the *sovereignty of God*, through recognition of His good, and wise, and holy *will*, as the true determining first cause of all events. We therefore say, that the distinctive of the Augustinian or Calvinistic system is not love, but sovereignty.

— *JAMES MACGREGOR (1888)*

1

INTRODUCTION

It is one of these unlikely stories, the story of the subject of this biography. It is hard to believe, humanly speaking, that one who began life in such humble surroundings in a small Perthshire town, and spent his early youth running about barefooted in highland dress and speaking the ancient tongue of the Celt should become a Professor in Theology in what was perhaps the foremost Divinity Hall of the day in Scotland.

Little is known of James MacGregor today. There is some information about him in the long out of print *Annals of the Free Church of Scotland, 1843-1900* (1914). More recently a brief article about him by Sherman Isbell appeared in the *Dictionary of Scottish Church History & Theology* (1993)[1] and a fuller piece by Ian Breward in the *Dictionary of New Zealand Biography* (1993).[2] An entry for MacGregor appeared in the centenary history of *New College, Edinburgh* by Hugh Watt, published in 1946, and brief mention is made of him in *Disruption and Diversity: Edinburgh Divinity 1846-1996* edited by David F. Wright and Gary D. Badcock (1996) in many ways a successor to the volume of Watt's.

---

[1] Mr Isbell's entry was largely based on an unpublished 45-page monograph produced by the present author in 1972. The current biographical sketch is an extensive re-writing and enlargement of the earlier monograph.

[2] Updated 12 November, 2013.

History, however, does not always deal well with great men. By any measure James MacGregor's story is a remarkable one. Not only from the point of view of his modest background, but also from the undeniable fact that he was an outstanding Christian theologian. His story, albeit belatedly, deserves to be told.

But what were the features of this man's life as a Christian minister and theologian, and why should his life and work be recalled and remembered at all? We mention here, briefly, four distinctive features of his ministerial life:

(1) *He was an outstanding theologian and defender of the faith*
MacGregor became a professor of divinity in New College, Edinburgh, the theological college of the Free Church of Scotland, one of the foremost Reformed Theological colleges of the day. He is recognisable as one of the school of the great Scottish theologian William Cunningham (1805-1861) whom he considered "the greatest master in theology Scotland ever produced,"[3] MacGregor had earlier written that in his view Cunningham was "the greatest divine that Scotland has produced."[4] He even named his second son after Cunningham! MacGregor was a staunch Calvinist throughout his life. For the greater part, on the disputed issues of the day he generally took a conservative line. It is recognised that this tended to put him at odds with theological trends in Scotland

[3] James MacGregor, *Studies in the History of Christian Apologetics*, Edinburgh, 1894, 195. [On the spine of this volume the title is given as *History of New Testament Apologetics*].
[4] James MacGregor, *Memorials of the late Rev. Henry M. Douglas*, Edinburgh, 1867, 16.

in the latter part of the nineteenth century, and later in New Zealand to where he immigrated in 1881.

(2) He was a prolific and stimulating writer[5]

He was one of the most prolific theological writers in the nineteenth century, when account is taken of all his contributions through books, pamphlets and religious periodicals in Scotland, New Zealand and the United States.[6] True, in some respects his style of writing was not especially elegant. But he did write with rare originality and erudition. One book reviewer said that "the author's style is extremely unpleasant and tantalising. No doubt you could not have the books without their style; for here if ever before, 'the style is the man.' But that does not lessen the irritation or weaken the earnestness of our wish that in order to be wiser he had striven to be less witty."[7] Nevertheless his work invariably is full of lively thought and well worth reading. It is arguable that MacGregor was responsible for two of the finest theological books of their kind to come out of the 19th century, his *Christian Doctrine* (1861) and *Sabbath Question* (1866). The book on Christian doctrine was written for youth and must be counted as one of the best summaries of Christian doctrine

---

[5] In *Disruption and Diversity* (Edinburgh, 1996), an authoritative history of theological training in Edinburgh between 1846 and 1996, George Newlands in the chapter on 'Divinity and Dogmatics' wrote that James MacGregor "appears to have written little" (p123). In reality MacGregor was quite a prolific writer, when account is also taken of pamphlets, magazine articles and publications during his time in New Zealand, as *Bibliography (A)* in this book attests (see pages 197ff below).

[6] See *Bibliography (A)*, in pages 197ff below.

[7] At the Literary Table. *The Expository Times*. Volume V. October, 1893 – September, 1894, 84. This is in a review of MacGregor's *The Revelation and the Record*, Edinburgh, 1893.

produced in that era. The other, on the question of the perpetuity of the 4th Commandment, also must be rated as one of the best treatments of the subject in that generation. Without question these books were decisive in his election by the Free Church as Professor of Systematic Theology in the New College in 1868.

(3) *He was a churchman of marked independent spirit.*

In the ecclesiastical scene he did become involved in many of the issues of the day. Very often he took an independent line. For example, he was on the anti-union side in the Union Controversy within the Free Church (1863-1872) though he subsequently supported the Mutual Eligibility proposals (1873) and the move for Disestablishment (1875). He took a strange position in the Case of William Robertson Smith, which disturbed the Free Church between 1877 and 1881.[8] He consistently claimed not to be a "party man." In a pamphlet written towards the end of his life MacGregor was to write: "I never belonged to any party in the Church, and I hope I never shall."[9] This independent spirit in some ways is summed up by the comment of one acquaintance: "There was about him...something...which gave to all his faculties a sweep and power and play that made everything he did and said his own, and not another's."[10] All this admittedly made him difficult to categorise within the ecclesiastical firmament of the day, though he was undoubtedly theologically conservative.

---

[8] See chapter 8 below.
[9] James MacGregor, *Freedom in the Truth*, Dunedin, 1890, 5.
[10] *The Christian Outlook*. No. 35, Vol. 1, October 20, 1894, 432.

(4) *He became one of the best-known theologians in Australasia*
MacGregor emigrated from Scotland to New Zealand in 1881. However, by his ministry and work there, he became, as one historian put it recently, "in his time, the best-known Presbyterian theologian in Australasia."[11] Though this move took him away from the 'mainstream' of theological life, he did become engaged in considerable 'local' debate, and it did see a period of very fruitful theological and controversial writing.[12] When he emigrated James MacGregor was in many ways at the peak of his powers, at just fifty-one years of age, after completing thirteen years as a Professor in New College. However, as one Obituary Notice of MacGregor stated after his death in 1894: "When Dr MacGregor accepted the pastorate in New Zealand, he did not cease to study theology, his mind remained active, and though in unfavourable circumstances, he did his utmost to keep abreast of advancing thought."[13] Ian Breward was to write of MacGregor's later ministry in New Zealand that "Corresponding widely with overseas theologians, he played an important part in debates in internationally read journals."

His story, therefore, is of considerable interest as he lived through a period of great change in the ecclesiastical and

[11] Ian Breward, 'MacGregor, James,' from *the Dictionary of New Zealand Biography*, Te Ara – the Encyclopedia of New Zealand, updated 12-Nov-2013 (http://www.TeAra.govt.nz/en/biographies/2m8/macgregor-james, accessed 27 March 2014).
[12] As his great trilogy on Apologetics penned at this time attest: *The Apology of the Christian Religion*, Edinburgh, 1891, 544pp; *The Revelation and the Record*, Edinburgh, 1893, xii+265pp; *Studies in the History of Christian Apologetics*, Edinburgh, 1894, ii+370pp.
[13] *The British Weekly*, Thursday, December 6th, 1894, No. 423 – Vol. XVII, 99

theological scene both in Scotland and New Zealand. This, then, is a tribute to an outstanding Reformed theologian. MacGregor is part of the heritage of the Reformed Faith in Scotland and New Zealand, and it is only right that this should be acknowledged.

It may be noted that this is an original piece of research. No biography was ever produced on James MacGregor. As far as is known, no doctoral theses have been written on his work and thought. The writer's interest in MacGregor first arose from some references in Principal John Macleod's *Scottish Theology* (1st edition, 1943). Macleod described him as "one of the school of Cunningham."[14] He also described him as "an expert in theological literature and in the realm of polemics."[15] Norman Macfarlane speaks of him as having "deep strains of genius,"[16] and R. Gordon Balfour in his 1899 Chalmers' Lectures entitled *Presbyterianism in the Colonies*, writes of MacGregor in this vein: "He was an amiable and accomplished man, a born theologian, with a keen sense of humour, a touch of real genius and more than a spark of celtic fire."[17]

In relation to the massive trilogy on Christian Apologetics which he wrote in New Zealand late in life, one reviewer says of them that "Dr MacGregor…has the ability (shall we say the genius?) to entitle him to range alongside the greatest of the Christian Apologists."[18] Praise indeed! B. B. Warfield of

---

[14] John Macleod, *Scottish Theology*, Edinburgh, ²1946, 250.

[15] ibid., 302.

[16] Norman C. Macfarlane, *Rev Donald John Martin*, Edinburgh, 1914, 34.

[17] R. G. Balfour, *Presbyterianism in the Colonies*, Edinburgh, 1899, 244.

[18] At the Literary Table. The Books of the Month. *The Expository Times*. Vol. III, October, 1891 – September, 1892, 136. This is in a review of

Princeton Theological Seminary, New Jersey, was to say of this trilogy that "the three volumes may well stand as his honourable monument, as they will, wherever they are read, powerfully advance the cause he had at heart."[19]

There is no question but that MacGregor was an "accomplished divine."[20] He became closely involved in discussions about Apologetics in his later life. Clearly there were huge issues facing the Church, and not least for those old school men, like MacGregor, who were "trained in the school of the strong, logical theology of a former age."[21] The tide was contrary in the last three decades of the nineteenth century. Liberalism, or Modernism, was in the ascendance. No doubt MacGregor's major works are considered in some respects to be dated. Nevertheless, he served his own generation by the will of God and sought to maintain historic Calvinism in a day when it became unpopular to do so. It is the writer's hope that this biography may do justice to the memory of this outstanding theologian, and be an encouragement in the present day to maintain the truth of an infallible Scripture, and to follow Christ as he sought to do.

One possible source of confusion requires to be put to rest here. In the 19th Century there were two prominent James MacGregor's within the Church scene in Scotland. One was a Free Churchman (after 1843 at least) – the subject of our study. He was born in 1829 (or 1830) and died, in New

---

MacGregor's *The Apology of the Christian Religion*, Edinburgh, 1891, a volume of 544 pages.

[19] Review in, *The Presbyterian and Reformed Review*, Vol. VIII, 1897, 772-773.

[20] J. S. Black & G. Chrystal, *The Life of William Robertson Smith*, Edinburgh, 1912, 102.

[21] *The Critical Review*, Vol. 5, 1895, 83.

Zealand, in 1894. The other James MacGregor was a Church of Scotland minister of the same name. His dates are very similar (1832-1910). This James MacGregor remained in the Church of Scotland and later became minister of St Cuthbert's Church in Edinburgh. Interestingly, these men both held charges, in their respective Churches, in the town of Paisley at the same time, one in the Free High Church and the other in the High Church (Established)! They had another likeness, too: they were both native Gaelic speakers. The Catalogue of the Union Seminary Library, New York City (1960), for one, confuses the two men.[22] Indeed, most theological library catalogues are guilty of the same confusion, as are some indices in historical studies.

---

[22] See Volume 6, Keo-Math, page 706 of the 1960 Edition. Care has to be taken in this connection in any searching on the Internet under "James MacGregor."

2

EARLY DAYS

Callander is a small town in the southern part of Perthshire. It is situated in beautiful countryside at the eastern fringes of the Trossachs. In recent times it has become in its own right a tourist centre, but it has retained much of its old-world attractiveness. It is situated on the River Teith near its junction with the Leny. Nearby are the scenic mountains enclosing Lochs Lubnaig to the north west and Venachar to the west. It is overshadowed by Ben Ledi ("The Hill of God"), a mountain just under 3,000 feet in height.

Callander is now a centre for tourism, but things were very different when James MacGregor was born there in 1829. It was MacGregor country of course, made famous by the exploits of "Rob Roy" MacGregor in the 18th Century. Rob Roy's base of operations was around Balquhidder, a small village some 12 miles north of Callander, situated at the eastern end of Loch Voil. Rob Roy is buried in the graveyard of the Old Kirk at Balquhidder, now a ruin. He died in 1734. James MacGregor had sweet memories of the place, of which he gave an account in a lecture entitled *Balquhidder, Rob Roy, &c.*, a lecture given to the Gaelic Society of Dunedin shortly after he emigrated from Scotland to New Zealand in 1881. He had known Balquhidder as a young boy, and on a visit in 1876 he noted that although it was near the borders of the

Lowlands, "it is at this hour a quiet Highland parish."[1] Callander, however, he found to be greatly changed: "In my boyhood there," he says, "it was a quiet Highland village: every-body spoke Gaelic, and we boys all wore the kilt."[2] Thirty years or so later, however, it was a different story: "But now it is a noisy, fashionable little lowland town. The Gaelic is no longer the language of the place." Amusingly he adds: "The kilt is seen only on imitation or artificial Celts – from London or elsewhere. All seems changed."[3] Nowadays, whilst the place is as pretty as ever, there is scarcely any semblance of Highland or Gaelic culture to be found there, apart from the inevitable souvenir shops!

James MacGregor was born in the "cross-street" in Callander on 6th January 1829. He was one of twins born to Duncan and Helen MacGregor. James's twin brother's name was Duncan Macpherson MacGregor. His mother's maiden name was Macpherson and his father was a builder in the area. The *Records of the Parish of Callander* record that the twins were born on 6th January, 1829.[4] A look at Parish Records indicates

---

[1] *Balquhidder, Rob Roy, &c.*, Dunedin, no date (circa 1882), 1. Dunedin, incidentally, is the Gaelic for Edinburgh. It appears that MacGregor had sought to have a record of his 1876 visit to his native area published in the *Blackwood* Magazine, a popular periodical of the 19th Century, produced from the offices of William Blackwood and Sons at 45 George Street, Edinburgh. (See the *Catalogue of Manuscripts Acquired since 1925* [National Library of Scotland]. Vol. III. Edinburgh, HMSO, 1968, MS4348 (Blackwood Papers 1805-1900, page 206)).

[2] ibid.

[3] ibid.

[4] *Old Parish Records* Births 336/00 0030 0016 (http://www.scotlandspeople.gov.uk/Search/results.aspx, accessed 27 March 2014). Interestingly, in the register of his marriage on 7th July, 1857, James MacGregor's age is given as 27. This implies a birth year of 1830. In

that James had many siblings. There is record of eight other children born to Duncan and Helen MacGregor: Margaret (1807), Angus (1809), Anne (1810), Duncan (1814), John (1816), Robert (1822), Donald (1824), and William (1826), ten in all including the twins.[5] Interestingly, MacGregor later recalled that "In my young days there were six James MacGregors in the little cross-street of Callander in which I was born."[6] All this makes the more remarkable the subsequent history of little "Jamie MacGregor" who was to become a notable minister and Professor beyond the limited environs of his youth.

In the days in which James MacGregor was born Callander was a town in a parish of some 2,000 inhabitants. There were around 320 houses and 450 families. "Both English and Gaelic languages are spoken in the parish," says the contemporary *Statistical Account* of the area, "and divine Worship on the Sabbath is performed in both. The name of almost every farm and hill is derived from the Gaelic. The

the *Annals of the Free Church of Scotland 1843-1900*, Vol. I, edited by the Rev. William Ewing, D.D., (Edinburgh, 1914), MacGregor's date of birth is given as 1830 (page 57). It is probably from this source that Hugh Watt has 1830 in his Centenary History of *New College Edinburgh* (Edinburgh, 1946, 229). There is a mistake somewhere and it is most likely to be on the register of marriage which should have had 28 as his age at the time of the marriage, unless there was a mistake in the Parish Records of births. However, it may be noted that his gravestone in Oamaru implies a birth-year of 1830. Curious.

[5] For a list of the offspring of Duncan and Helen MacGregor see http://wc.rootsweb.ancestry.com/cgi-bin/igm.cgi?op=AHN&db=robinp&id=I01280 (accessed 27 March 2014). In a conversation with the author in London on Tuesday 4th May 1971, Mrs Margaret Patrick, a grand-daughter of James MacGregor's, said he was reputed to be the last of fifteen children, but that seems to be overstated.

[6] James MacGregor, *Balquhidder, Rob Roy, &c.*, Dunedin, (1882), 8.

Highland dress is not so generally worn as it was forty years ago." As far as the social life was concerned, the reporter recorded that, "The people are in general well informed, intelligent, sober in their habits, kind and affectionate in their dispositions, and upon the whole, moral, religious, and well disposed."[7] As for his own family situation, it may safely be assumed that he was raised in a God-fearing home where the ordinances of public worship were faithfully observed and in which family worship would have been conducted morning and evening. Most likely the worship in the home, at least in James's earliest days, would have been in Gaelic, the head of the home asking the blessing on the worship, singing a Psalm and reading a portion of Scripture, before committing the whole family to the Lord for the day or night.

It is clear that the traditions in Callander were evangelical on the whole. The Church of Scotland minister before the Disruption of May 1843 was understood to sympathise with the Evangelical party, though when the crunch came he resigned his charge rather than enter the Free Church. However, a considerable majority of the congregation formed a Free Church congregation, including the MacGregor family. In an address given in Columba Church, Oamaru, on 28th May 1893, James MacGregor recalled an account of the Disruption in the *Edinburgh Witness* of 19th May 1843: "It was in the hands of a woman, the centre of an excited group, such that I, a very small boy, was drawn in by fascination of the excitement. Another woman, the daughter of an elder, copious in

---

[7] *Statistical Account of Scotland. Perth.* Vol. X. Parish of Callander. (Report by the Rev. P. Robertson, Minister). William Blackwood and Sons, Edinburgh & London, 1845, 349ff. The account refers to the year 1831.

eloquence, went on declaiming about the folly of some people. The one who held the newspaper…went on pointing to that column of the paper…throwing in the words: *Ach tha ceithir chidan dhiubh ann* (but there are 400 of them)."[8]

For a time the Free Church congregation worshiped in the Independent Chapel or in the open air. A site for a Church was obtained from one Donald M'Laren, who had initially been hostile to the Free Church. He had a change of mind, however, and in due time he granted a site on easy conditions in a beautiful spot near the river.[9] A new Free Church was built in 1843-44, no doubt with the practical assistance of James MacGregor's father. A Free Church School was begun in 1843 and a large School building was opened in 1849. This building is still to be seen, much as it was, in Church Street, alongside the much-altered former Free Church building.[10]

In 1848 there were 382 members in the Free Church congregation in Callander. Until 1857 the Church was bi-lingual, in English and Gaelic. The first minister was Duncan McLean (1805-1858) who was translated from Kilmodan

---

[8] Quoted in Peter Matheson, *The Finger of God in the Disruption*, Alexandra, New Zealand, 1993, 28.

[9] T. Brown, *Annals of the Disruption*, Edinburgh, 1893, 471-2.

[10] Prior to 1843, before the establishment in Scotland of a state-provided school system (1872), children who did attend schools would generally have gone to the local Assembly, or Parish, School or an entirely private School. The education, broadly speaking, would have been based on the three r's: reading, writing and arithmetic. It would have been a good basic education in English, even in Gaelic speaking areas. By 1847 the Free Church had established around 500 Schools of its own together with two teacher training Colleges (in Glasgow and Edinburgh). See Norman L. Walker, *Chapters from the History of the Free Church of Scotland*, Edinburgh, 1895, 113-129.

(Argyll) in 1844. Mr McLean suffered greatly at the time of the Disruption, but he had a happy ministry in Callander, although his health was not good and he resigned the charge in 1857 at the age of only 52.[11] He had a daughter, Grace, who had been born in 1834. James MacGregor must first have met Grace when her father was translated to Callander towards the end of 1844. They would have known one another in the Church of course, and also very likely at the School before James went off to Edinburgh University in 1847.

The schoolmasters of those days exercised considerable influence over their charges, academically, and also very often spiritually. In James MacGregor's early and mid-teens the 'dominie' was one Thomas Lillie, who was appointed in 1845 to the Free Church Day School. It was said of Lillie that "he had rare powers of communicating knowledge, stimulating thought, and influencing the lives of youths for all that was noble and true." James MacGregor at least must have been one of his most responsive pupils. It seems that Lillie devoted his Sabbath evenings to the instruction of young people in the Bible, and we can believe that this is where James MacGregor may even have been converted at that time, and acquired a good grounding in Scripture truth and basic Reformed doctrine.[12] It is very likely that Grace McLean attended such gatherings, and it may be that the first sparks were lit there which led in 1857 to James and Grace being joined as man and wife.

---

[11] The story of Duncan McLean's trials is told at length in Thomas Brown's *Annals of the Disruption*, 393-398.
[12] D. McMartin, *A Short History of the United Free Church, Callander*, Edinburgh, c1908, 5-10.

James MacGregor's upbringing was a humble one. In an Obituary Notice in the *Oamaru Mail* of Monday, October 8th, 1894, it was said that "his parentage was humble, and he faced life only with a big ambition and an empty purse," and it was only by "sheer dogged persistence, the strictest economy, and the hardest of unceasing effort that he won his way to college and laid the foundation of his successful career." Over and above all this, it is reasonable to believe that by then he was trusting in the Lord, and knew that from however humble a background, the believer can say: "I can do all things through Christ which strengtheneth me" (Philippians 4:13). He surely believed that, whatever his disadvantages, if God were with him he need not be intimidated by the greatest odds against him.

Principal William Cunningham

3

STUDENT IN EDINBURGH

It must have been quite a thought for a boy in his mid-teens to go up to Edinburgh for an Arts course. Young men went to University at a very early age in those days and no doubt it could be a maturing experience, or else it would be quite a harrowing one.

James MacGregor studied Arts at Edinburgh University between 1847 and 1851. He was a diligent student with a particular aptitude for Logic and Moral Philosophy. A fellow student, James Freer (1829-1887), knew James MacGregor from the time he went up to Edinburgh University. "He was," said Freer, "throughout his entire academical course, a most diligent and successful student. While occupying a high position in all his classes, he took a foremost place in logic and moral philosophy."[1] Why MacGregor had such a penchant for philosophical subjects is hard to say. It may be that speculative thought is a distinct characteristic of the Celt or Highlander. This must at least have appealed to him. It carried over to the New College course in which there were classes in Moral Philosophy conducted by Patrick C. MacDougall (1806-1867). MacDougall was Professor of Moral Philosophy in New College from 1844 to 1853 but in 1850

---

[1] *Proceedings and Debates of the General Assembly of the Free Church of Scotland* (hereafter, *PDGAFCS*), May 1868, 215.

had been appointed to the same position in the University of Edinburgh.

It seems clear that MacDougall had a profound influence on young MacGregor both at the University and New College. He said of the young student that "He carried off the highest honours of his year, and his essays were in a high degree remarkable for the originality, vigour, and logical acuteness displayed in them."[2] Another fellow student of MacGregor's was the future Professor of Logic and Rhetoric in the University of Glasgow, James Veitch. "He stood out then," said Veitch, "as one of the men of highest intellectual mark in the (New) College. He was especially distinguished for logical power, clearness, depth, consecutiveness, and subtlety. These qualities were displayed whatever might be the subject to which his mind was applied. His capacity for the abstract investigations of the metaphysical department of philosophy were hardly less remarkable than his logical power."[3] MacGregor graduated Master of Arts in 1851.[4]

Whatever James MacGregor's liking for philosophical studies may have been, his primary concern in going up to New College was to prepare for the ministry of the Free Church. At what point in his experience he became conscious of a call to the ministry, we have no real means of now knowing. It may be assumed, although it is only a speculation, that this was something to which encouragement was given to

---

[2] ibid.

[3] ibid.

[4] Ian Breward, 'MacGregor, James,' from *the Dictionary of New Zealand Biography*, Te Ara — the Encyclopedia of New Zealand, updated 12-Nov-2013 (http://www.TeAra.govt.nz/en/biographies/2m8/macgregor-james, accessed 27 March 2014).

him by Duncan McLean in Callander, or perhaps the local 'Dominie,' Thomas Lillie. It may be, however, that such a call into the ministry of the Word came to him under the influential ministry of the Rev. John Bruce in St Andrew's Free Church, then located at 80 George Street in the west end of the New Town of the city. It may be, indeed, that it was under Bruce's ministry that he experienced a saving change in the first place, and then subsequently the call to the ministry. At any rate James MacGregor came under the oversight of the Edinburgh Presbytery and embarked upon the normal four-year divinity course at New College in November 1851. He was one of 54 students who entered the College in that 1851-2 Session. This was the first year in which the building designed by W. H. Playfair, erected at the top of the Mound, was used

PLAYFAIR'S PLAN, NEW COLLEGE

for classes. The building was to become a prominent feature of the Edinburgh skyline.

In his Centenary History of New College Hugh Watt reproduces the announcement of the College classes for the 1851-2 Session.[5] The following are the details of the courses that year:

[5] Hugh Watt, *New College Edinburgh, A Centenary History*, Edinburgh, 1946, 30-31.

NEW COLLEGE

The *CLASSES* for the ensuing *WINTER* will Meet in the *NEW BUILDING* at the Head of the *MOUND*, and the *SESSION* will be OPENED there upon *TUESDAY*, the 4th NOVEMBER next, at TWO o'clock P.M., when an ADDRESS will be delivered by

The Rev. *WILLIAM CUNNINGHAM*, D.D., *Principal*

The CLASSES for the different Branches of Study will be opened as follows:–

Classes.	Days and Hours of Attendance.	Professors.
Divinity		
Junior Class	Wednesday, November 5, *One* o'clock.	DR BUCHANAN, 51 Lauriston Place.
Senior Class	Ditto, *Eleven* o'clock.	
Divinity		
Junior Class	Wednesday, November 5, *One* o'clock.	DR BANNERMAN, 7 Clarendon Crescent.
Senior Class	Ditto, *Eleven* o'clock.	
Divinity and Church History		
Junior Class	Wednesday, November 5, *Eleven* o'clock.	DR CUNNINGHAM, 17 Salisbury Road.
Senior Class	Ditto, *One* o'clock.	
Hebrew and Oriental Languages		
Junior Class	Wednesday, November 5, *Twelve* o'clock.	DR DUNCAN, 6 Frederick Street.
Senior Class	Ditto, *Ten* o'clock.	
Exegetical Theology		
Junior Class	Wednesday, November 5, *Twelve* o'clock.	DR BLACK, 16 Claremont Crescent.
Senior Class	Ditto, *Ten* o'clock.	
Natural Science, with Excursions	Wednesday, November 5, *Two* o'clock.	Professor FLEMING, 22 Walker Street.
Moral Philosophy		
Lectures	Wednesday, November 5, *Twelve* o'clock.	Professor MACDOUGALL 38 Great King Street.
Examinations and Exercises	Ditto, *Two* o'clock	
Logic and Metaphysics		
Lectures	Wednesday, November 5, *One* o'clock.	Professor FRASER, Greenhill Gardens.
Examinations and Exercises .	Ditto, *Three* o'clock.	

According to these arrangements, the Curriculum for Students of Theology will stand thus:–

First Year's Students

Attend   Dr DUNCAN's Junior Class at *Twelve*.

Dr BANNERMAN's do. at *One*.

Dr FLEMING's Class at *Two*.

Second Year's Students

Attend   Dr DUNCAN's Senior Class at *Ten.*

Dr CUNNINGHAM's Junior Class at *Eleven.*

Dr BUCHANAN's do. at *One.*

Third Year's Students

Attend   Dr BUCHANAN's Senior Class at *Eleven.*

Dr BLACK's Junior Class at *Twelve.*

Dr CUNNINGHAM's Senior Class at *One.*

Fourth Year's Students

Attend   Dr BLACK's Senior Class at *Ten.*

Dr BANNERMAN's do. at *Eleven.*

The Rev. THEO. MEYER will open a Class for Hebrew at *Nine* o'clock.

MATRICULATION. Students of Theology, before entering with the Professors, must matriculate in the Library, and pay the common fee to the Secretary of the College.

Admission to the Classes of the New College is not limited to Students qualifying for the Ministry, or connected with the Free Church of Scotland.

JAMES BONAR, Secretary to the College.

NEW COLLEGE, EDINBURGH,
3ᵈ September 1851.

When James MacGregor went up to New College for divinity studies in 1851 it was to a faculty of unparalleled strength from the standpoint of the older orthodoxy. The Principal was William Cunningham (1805-1861), who occupied the chair of Church History. James Buchanan (1804-1870) was in the Chair of Divinity (later Systematic Theology), and James Bannerman (1807-1868) also taught Divinity (later called Apologetics, Christian Ethics and Pastoral Theology). John Duncan – "Rabbi" Duncan (1796-1870) – was in the Chair of Hebrew and Oriental Languages, and Alexander Black (1789-1864) was the Professor of Exegetical Theology (essentially New Testament Language and Literature). This constituted an outstanding Senatus. Without question the teaching he received under these men was influential in forming the thinking and theological commitment of the young James MacGregor. At that point in the history of the Free Church there was no whiff of the sort of liberalism or Biblical Criticism which was later largely to destroy its clear testimony to an infallible Scripture and old-school Calvinism.

In his later life MacGregor was to say this of the early Free Church Professors: "What a theological faculty the Disruption Church was able to extemporise in her birth year! There is not one of the four [Thomas Chalmers, David Welsh, John Duncan and Alexander Black] that was not, in his own independent way, a true master, essentially unique in British history of Christian thought; and surely such a combination in one theological school has rarely appeared in Christian history." With reference to his own experience at New College, MacGregor was to go on to say this: "The present writer may be allowed to make this observation as having been personally a pupil of Cunningham and Duncan. In such labours as the present he has been always deeply indebted to the tuition of Dr. Bannerman, who had come to be their colleague, – represented in literature by his books on Inspiration and on The Church, – who, like Dr. James Buchanan, was of the type of that 'first four' in respect of maturity of rich thought and belief, and clear, solid strength of judgement, as well as affluence of digested and really mastered knowledge of his subjects."[6]

MacGregor's appreciation for Cunningham knew no bounds. It is clear that this was the most enduring influence on his theological understanding. In later years when he was Professor of Systematic Theology at the same College, as we shall see, he did not hesitate to use his mentor's *Historical Theology*, which in essence represented lectures he himself received in his College days.[7]

The young student's learning soon became evident when in his second year at New College he published a substantial pamphlet entitled *Three Smooth Stones from the Brook*.[8] This amounted to a defence of the rationale for the Disruption and in his presentation he showed a keen awareness of Church issues of the day.

---

[6] James MacGregor, *Studies in the History of Christian Apologetics*, Edinburgh, 1894, 307.
[7] *PDGAFCS*, May 1871. Report XXVII on the Quinquennial Visitation of New College, 11. Cunningham's *Historical Theology* (2 volumes) was first published posthumously in 1862. It was reprinted by the Banner of Truth Trust in 1960 and remains in print (2015).
[8] James MacGregor, *Three Smooth Stones from the Brook: A Brief Exhibition of the Case of Mr James Lamont, the Case of the Free Church of Scotland, and the Case of the Church Established in Scotland*, Edinburgh, 1853, 51pp.

Whilst at New College, MacGregor was apparently a great debater. "In the debating society connected with the (New) College he had no superior; and in every discussion in which he took part, he displayed great vigour and acuteness of mind, as well as a wide range of information."[9] MacGregor himself states that the debates of the *Metaphysical and Ethical Society* "contributed more to their intellectual development than all other academical influences together."[10] On the more spiritual side, MacGregor speaks of the Friday meetings for prayer conducted by the Professors and the Saturday meetings of the *Students' Missionary Association* as special sources of blessing.[11]

In later years MacGregor told of a lesson he learned at College from Professor Duncan. He had made some remark about the irksomeness of acquiring knowledge, of learning and remembering a number of facts. "No," said the Professor, "that is not knowledge. Knowledge is not irksome. Knowledge is simply *seeing* things, and the pursuit of knowledge is just like climbing a hill. As you ascend you see things that are hidden from those beneath."[12] It appears, however, that not only was James MacGregor an outstanding student and an omnivorous reader, he also "had a memory of extraordinary retentiveness," which no doubt stood him in good stead throughout his student days as well as his subsequent ministry.

In his student days in Edinburgh, as we have indicated, MacGregor attended on the ministry of the Rev. John Bruce

---

[9] *PDGAFCS*, May 1868, 215. (James Freer).
[10] James MacGregor, *Memorials of the late Rev. Henry M. Douglas*, Edinburgh, 1867, 15.
[11] ibid., 16.
[12] *The Christian Outlook*. No. 35, Vol. 1, October 20, 1894, 432.

at Free St Andrew's, in the West End of the New Town, though it appears that in his first year at New College (1851-2) MacGregor attended the ministry of the Rev. William King Tweedie (1803-1863) at the Tolbooth Free Church.[13] He would unquestionably have enjoyed an edifying and spiritual ministry at St Andrew's and the Tolbooth Free Churches. Bruce (1794-1880) was one of the preachers in Edinburgh in those days whose ministry, according to Principal John Macleod, "was blessed to the conversion and upbuilding of students for the ministry; and the conversion of these young men who attended with a revived and deepened and abiding interest not only in the practical everyday Evangel which they faithfully proclaimed, but the whole circle of Christian truth."[14] In later years MacGregor was to contribute an appreciation of Bruce in the *Disruption Worthies*.[15] James MacGregor finished his New College course in 1855 and was licensed by the Presbytery of Edinburgh later that year.

---

[13] Up to May 1852 Tolbooth Free Church was housed in the old Original Secession Church in Infirmary Street near the South Bridge in the east end of the city, before moving for worship to the Music Hall in George Street until a new Church building was opened in the north side of St Andrew's Square in May 1858. It is assumed that the Infirmary Street building was nearer to MacGregor's residence in 1851-52.

[14] John Macleod, *Scottish Theology*, Edinburgh, ²1946, 257.

[15] *Disruption Worthies – A Memorial of 1843*, Edinburgh, 1881, 79-86.

4

FREE CHURCH MINISTRY

Licensed by the Edinburgh Free Church Presbytery in 1855, James MacGregor preached his first sermon, as a licensed minister, in his home congregation of Callander. An eager congregation apparently thronged the Church there to suffocation point to hear that sermon. His fellow towns-people had mingled feelings of pride and curiosity at this first of their sons to enter the ministry. After all, this was young Jamie MacGregor from the local builder's large family. "And right well, the story runs, were they gratified, for the young divine preached a sermon which is talked of to this day in the little Scotch town by those who have since watched with pride the making of their own townsman's name in the theological and literary world."[1]

After his licensing in 1855 MacGregor became assistant minister in Uddingston, then a small town to the south east of Glasgow in Lanarkshire. A Free Church Mission had been started there by the Bothwell minister, John Buchanan, in 1854. MacGregor was not long at Uddingston as within two years he was called by the Free Church congregation in Barry, Forfarshire, near the South Angus coast, to which he was ordained early in 1857. Barry was a small village inland on the road between Monifieth to the south-west and Carnoustie to

---

[1] Obituary Notice in the *Oamaru Mail* of Monday October 8, 1894.

the north-east. The congregation was a small one, numbering 200 or so members. The minister and many of the people had come out at the Disruption and shortly thereafter a Church and manse were built. The vacancy had arisen because the Disruption minister, the Rev. James Lumsden (1810-1875) had in 1856 been called by the Church to the Chair of Systematic Theology in the Aberdeen Free Church College. And so the call from Barry eventually came to James MacGregor.

Shortly after he was ordained and inducted to the congregation at Barry, he was married to Grace Campbell McLean in Callander on 7th July 1857 by the Rev. Donald Fergusson, Free Church minister from nearby Kilmadock (Doune).[2] By this time James's father had passed on, but his mother and many of his wider family were resident in Callander. From this happy union there were in the course of time 10 children born, three of whom died of *tuberculosis* in their youth, but several of his daughters lived into old age, the youngest of whom, Charlotte, survived into her nineties and passed away in 1966, the last of his surviving children. In fact concern of the health of his family was a reason, as we shall see, for his resignation from New College and subsequent immigration to New Zealand in 1881.

MacGregor had a happy ministry of nearly four years in Barry. Besides the preaching and pastoral duties, the young minister gave himself to study. He took full opportunity of being in a relatively small and quiet charge. In his time in Barry he produced the first of his significant publications. It

---

[2] Marriages in the Parish of Callander in the County of Perth. 1857. Entry 5. Page 3.

was a book for youth on *Christian Doctrine*. This book had the sub-title, "A Text-Book for Youth." In effect it was a compendium of theology and it received high praise such as the following high recommendation from prominent evangelical ministers of the day:

> "We have pleasure in calling the attention of ministers and teachers of Bible classes to the admirable text-book of Christian Doctrine recently published by Mr Elliot.[3] In the comprehensiveness of its plan, the precision of its statements, and the fullness and appropriateness of its scriptural proofs, it seems to us to be far superior to any work of the kind with which we are acquainted."
>
> (Signed) ROB. S. CANDLISH, D.D., Edinburgh; JOHN ROBSON, D.D., Glasgow; WILLIAM CUNNINGHAM, D.D., New College, Edinburgh; JAMES BEGG, D.D., Edinburgh; ANDREW THOMSON, D.D., Edinburgh; JULIUS WOOD, D.D., Dumfries.

In a notice of the book in the *British and Foreign Evangelical Review* of 1861, Professor George Smeaton of New College, Edinburgh, described it as "a most admirable manual for those who wish to be introduced into a systematic view of divine truth in a condensed form, and also for those who have occasion to instruct others in the Christian system." The book no doubt emerged from his ministerial labours in Barry. The date appended to the initial printing was 23rd February 1861. It went through twelve printings of a thousand copies each between 1861 and 1874. In the final printing in 1874 it

---

[3] This has reference to the Edinburgh Publisher, Andrew Elliot of 15 Princes Street.

amounted to 168 pages. More recently Ian Breward has described this book as "a skilful popularisation of Calvinist theology."[4]

The content is thoroughly Calvinistic. With reference to the decree of God, the author says: "In the origin and history of the universe, everything proceeds upon a plan, or decree, pre-existing in the mind of God. This plan or decree is variously described in Scripture as the 'good pleasure,' the 'counsel,' the 'purpose,' the 'predestination' of God. It embraces all that comes to pass, in time and through eternity; God 'worketh *all things* after the counsel of his own will,' (Eph. i.11)."[5] Even the fall of man into sin is foreordained: "The fall of man had been foreseen from eternity. From eternity the Creator had arranged a method, and provided the means, of restoration, (Eph. i. 4.) So that, when the enemy had prevailed in his temptation, and man was fallen, and paradise was lost, God had but to execute His eternal decree, to employ the means eternally provided, in order that the enemy should be baffled, and man restored, and paradise regained."[6] Man is totally depraved: "The race of men is miserable and depraved. And under the government of a just God, this can be accounted for only by the truth that the race of men is guilty, that they have contracted guilt, incurred God's wrath, in Adam's first sin. Because in Adam all have sinned, therefore 'in Adam all die,' (1 Cor. xv. 22.)...(Rom. v.

[4] Ian Breward, 'MacGregor, James,' from *the Dictionary of New Zealand Biography*, Te Ara – the Encyclopedia of New Zealand, updated 12-Nov-2013 (http://www.TeAra.govt.nz/en/biographies/2m8/macgregor-james, accessed 27 March 2014).
[5] James MacGregor, *Christian Doctrine*, Edinburgh, 1874, 24.
[6] ibid., 58.

12.)"[7] Salvation for any of the sinful sons of Adam is entirely of free sovereign grace: "...*electing love is free and sovereign*. – It is an 'election of grace,' (Rom. xi. 5.). God has been determined in His choice wholly and solely by His own 'good pleasure,' even as He 'works all things after the counsel of His own will.' (Eph. i. 5, 9, 11.) He has chosen His people freely and unconditionally, as a sovereign, giving His electing love to whom He will, in what measure He will, because He wills it."[8] This predestination is to the glory of God: "The chief end of man is to glorify God: the only conceivable end of God, or purpose of His working, is to glorify Himself: 'He hath made all things for Himself, yea, even the wicked for the day of evil,' (Prov. xvi. 4.) He has predestined his own people: 'according to the good pleasure of His will, to the praise of the glory of His grace,' (Eph. i. 5, 6.)"[9] But how are people's sins paid for? How are sinners redeemed? "The Lord took on Himself the burden of our guilt, endured the wrath of God which our sin deserved, and completed His suffering by dying in our room, a painful, shameful, and accursed death upon the cross. (John x. 11; Phil. ii. 6-9; 1 Peter ii. 24; Gal. iii. 13.) The effect of His deed of redeeming love is, that the justice of God is satisfied, the sin of His people is atoned for, their lost life is redeemed, – they are guiltless, righteous, accepted, – their salvation is immutably secured in Him, (Rom. viii. 32-39; 2 Cor. v. 21; Eph. i. 7; Acts xx. 28; 1 Peter i. 18, 19.)"[10] But how are those whom the Father has elected and for whom the Son has died,

---

[7] ibid., 54.

[8] ibid., 60-61.

[9] ibid., 24.

[10] ibid., 76.

to come into possession of this salvation? The answer is, by the inward work of the Holy Spirit: "The Spirit of grace renews, and sanctifies, and glorifies, all those, and only those whom the Father has chosen, (Acts xviii. 48; 2 Tim. i. 9,) whom the Son has redeemed, (Ps. cx. 3; John x. 14, 26-28.)"[11] "As distinguished from the mere outward call of the word, there is an inward, efficacious call of the Spirit by the word, the call of God's elect, (Rom. viii. 30; 2 Peter i. 10.) They, in God's time, are made 'alive from the dead,' in order that they may gladly leave their sins, and turn to God in Christ, (1 Cor. ii. 12; Ps. cx. 3.)"[12] This work of the Spirit ensures the perseverance of the saved: "no one who is really renewed by the Spirit, who has exercised a saving faith upon the Son, can ever be lost, (Isa. xl. 30, 31; Ps. xxxvii. 23, 24.)...The life which is put forth in faith is in its nature immortal; the Spirit, whose grace enables the sinner to believe, is in His purposes unchangeable, 'His gifts and calling are without repentance,' (Rom. xi. 29.)"[13] There is little doubt that the small rural congregation in Barry was treated to an expository and doctrinal ministry of unusual richness.

A prominent periodical of the day, the *News of the Churches* had this to say about MacGregor's *Text Book for Youth*:

> The first thing that strikes the most cursory reader of this curious little book of some 164 small octavo pages, is the extraordinary amount of matter which the writer has contrived to press into its pages. The style in which it is written, besides, is condensed and yet free, close and yet open and

[11] ibid., 83.
[12] ibid., 87.
[13] ibid., 94.

graceful. The vigour and grasp displayed in his conception of the three parts of the 'Doctrine of Nature,' 'Grace, the Gift of God,' and 'Grace, the Duty of Man,' are as remarkable as the spirit and energy with which the outlines are filled up.

James and Grace MacGregor in 1862 with (from the left) William, Georgina and Duncan.

Early in 1861 MacGregor received a call to a considerably more demanding situation in Paisley. The previous minister, the Rev. John B. Dickson, after a ministry of seven years, resigned the charge in 1859. A standard history of the town takes up the story: "The Free High Church congregation then elected Mr. James McGregor, who was inducted on 30th April, 1861."[14] At the time MacGregor went to Paisley the membership (that is to say all adults and children, communicant members or otherwise) numbered about 1,000 souls. As to his ministry in Paisley, one of his congregation, Dr William Brunton, rector of Paisley Grammar School and an elder in the congregation, was to say this:

> The first time I saw him and heard his voice was in the little church at Barry, with a brother elder. I had gone there for the purpose of hearing him. I soon felt deeply interested in the man, and in his thorough manner of handling the subjects of discourse. There was something so original, simple, and impressive in the whole service that I felt that this is the man whose ministrations I should like to attend. The Free High Church congregation was in a very unsettled state when he was called to it; indeed, it required very great courage in a minister to undertake the responsibility of soothing down party feelings, and of bringing the congregation into harmonious working. In a few months, by faithful preaching, conciliatory and faithful manners, and great wisdom in managing affairs, Mr. MacGregor was not only the means of putting all right again, but, with the cordial help of the

---

[14] Robert Brown, *The History of Paisley*, Volume II. Paisley, 1886, 360.

office-bearers and others, new schemes of usefulness were undertaken…[15]

"I have met with no man more scholarly than Mr McGregor," Dr Brunton continued, "none who has read so much of ancient and modern literature, who has such a command of ancient and modern tongues. He is perfectly familiar with Greek and Latin, and with the literature of both Greece and Rome…I speak in the highest terms of him as an expounder of the Word of God and a preacher of the gospel – as a man and a minister – as one who is never idle, but always acquiring."[16]

One of the issues James MacGregor took up in his time in Paisley was the Sabbath question. There was considerable pressure for change, not least coming from sources within the Established Church. The traditional respect for the Lord's day as the Christian Sabbath was being eroded, partly under the supposed demands of the Industrialising society, not least around Glasgow and the west. In the forefront of the weakening of the theology of the Sabbath were the prominent Established Church men Dr Norman Macleod of the Barony Church in the city, and Principal John Tulloch of St Andrews, who had been appointed Editor of the *Church of Scotland Record* in 1861. There was with these influential men an incipient denial of the perpetuity of the Fourth Commandment and an evident desire to relax its authority and obligations. MacGregor, exercised by what was happening, took up the defence of the Sabbath and produced a work of outstanding

[15]   See   http://nzetc.victoria.ac.nz/tm/scholarly/tei-Stout65-t21.html (accessed 13th January, 2015).
[16] *PDGAFCS*, Edinburgh, May 1868, 215.

quality entitled, *The Sabbath Question, Historical, Scriptural, and Practical.*[17] John Macleod says this of the book and its author: "The champion who took up his [Dr Norman Macleod's] challenge and who produced another work worthy of the traditions of Scottish Theology was the brilliant, though erratic, James MacGregor. His book on the Sabbath Question deals with Norman's teaching as only an expert in theological literature and in the realm of polemics could handle it. It is conclusive in argument, vigorous in style, and has in it a bite that is almost the hallmark of that streak of genius which is found in the author's work."[18] The sad fact was, however, that "the social standing such as that of a court chaplain and personal popularity such as his opponent had told mightily in the direction of furthering the abandonment of Orthodox ideas in the subject of what had been a leading feature of distinctly Scottish religious life."[19]

In relation to Norman Macleod's denial of the perpetuity of the Sabbath commandment, MacGregor says this: "He finds himself, *therefore*, constrained in conscience publicly to deny it, though it be the doctrine and law of his Church. This, of course, is no new thing. A minister may any day find himself at variance with the doctrine of his Church, and on this ground seek to be relieved of her ministry, because he can no longer discharge its duties. But the peculiarity in Dr Macleod's position is this, that while denying and assailing the Church's doctrine *he retains her ministry*; he retains an office after he has avowedly become unable to discharge its duties;

---

[17] Edinburgh: Duncan Grant, 1866, xii + 433pp.
[18] John Macleod, *Scottish Theology*, Edinburgh, ²1946, 302.
[19] ibid.

he continues to accept wages after he has avowedly become unable to do the work for which he is paid. And while occupying a position so painful to contemplate, he appears to claim credit for a peculiar measure of ingenuous honesty, almost for a baby-like simplicity and integrity of purpose! Of the *moral* aspect of this position, I need not say a word. But as to its bearing on the question of his trustworthiness as a religious guide, a leader in his church, the editor of *Good Words*, I feel warranted in quoting the warning words of the great Apostle whom the reverend Doctor quotes on the topic of 'liberality:' 'Now I beseech you, brethren, mark them which cause divisions and offences contrary to the doctrine you have learned, and avoid them. For they that are such serve not our Lord Jesus Christ, but their own belly: and by *good words* and *fair speeches* deceive the hearts of the simple.' (Rom. xvi. 17, 18)."[20] Sadly, the sort of attitude of Norman Macleod was to become endemic increasingly in the Presbyterian Churches in Scotland so that on many issues the pass was sold, and Biblical truth denied and undermined, all in the interests supposedly of a 'liberty' and progressiveness, which, however, was to be a deadly legacy to the church of the twentieth century.

But what can true-hearted Christians do in the face of such change and decay? MacGregor counsels wisely: "to those who love the truth, the Primitive Church teaches a most important lesson. She shows us that if we would have our children to become unconsciously imbued with the high doctrine, we must accustom them from infancy to the high practice, teaching them by precept and example to follow in the footsteps of the saints of old, under both Testaments,

---

[20] James MacGregor, *The Sabbath Question*, Edinburgh, 1866, 41-42.

'Calling the Sabbath a delight, holy of the Lord, honourable.'
The same practice on our part will set us in the right point of
view, the proper frame of mind and heart, both for the
recognition of the true doctrine and for the due appreciation
of the truth, – that 'jewel of great price,' – when found. And a
thorough-going practice of the truth, like the practice of the
Puritans and primitive Church, is that which will, next to
God's own Word, most impressively commend it to the
acceptance of God-fearing individuals, families, and
communities which have not yet attained to the God-given
truth in its fullness of life-giving light. … the most effective
answer to the popular objections to the Sabbath prescribed by
God's Word is a due observance and enjoyment of that
Sabbath by God's people."[21]

This is the teaching his dear people in Paisley were to be
exposed to. "There is no part of the book," he says in the
Preface, "available for pastoral instruction that had not, in the
class-room or from the pulpit, been addressed to the
congregation in which I am minister."[22] Indeed, the book is
dedicated to "The Office-bearers, Members, and Adherents of
the Free High Church, Paisley," as a "Memorial and Fruit of
Pastoral Labours among them." Some of it had previously
appeared in sound evangelical periodicals for which he had
begun to produce material, such as *The Family Treasury*, and
The British and Foreign Evangelical Review.

It was quite clear that in James MacGregor the
congregation at Paisley had a divine of unusual ability. This
was soon recognised by the wider Church and when Dr James

---

[21] ibid., 367-8.
[22] ibid., v.

Buchanan retired from the Chair of Systematic Theology at New College in 1868, MacGregor's name inevitably came to the fore as an appropriate successor. He was duly elected to the Chair by the General Assembly of May 1868. However, on leaving Paisley he was "entertained at a public dinner in the George Hotel on 27th October 1868, Provost Macfarlane presiding."[23]

---

[23] Robert Brown, op. cit., 361.

5

UNION CONTROVERSY

From the earliest days when he went into print as a student, James MacGregor tended to take up controversial themes. Whilst still a student in 1853 he took issue with a writer who questioned the validity of the Disruption of 1843 and the continuing separate existence of the Free Church.[1] Shortly after he began his ministry he entered the fray in the matter of the "Glasgow College Case," a matter brought in to the Assembly of 1859 through the College Committee. It involved accusations on the part of the Professor of Systematic Theology in the Glasgow College against some of his students whom he considered, among other things, to be defective in their view of the doctrine of total depravity. To him they conceded far too much ability to natural man in understanding of the truth of God. The case came up to the General Assembly of 1859, and MacGregor, as a member of Assembly that year, felt a responsibility to make his opinions on the matter known.

In this instance he took part with the students against their Professor (James Gibson) and in the process produced a pamphlet revealing considerable learning entitled *A Vindication of Natural Theology, on grounds of Reason, Scripture, and Orthodoxy;*

---

[1] See *Three Smooth Stones from the Brook: or, a brief Exhibition of the Case of Mr James Lamont, the Case of the Free Church of Scotland, and the Case of the Church Established in Scotland*, Edinburgh, 1853.

with special reference to the Glasgow College Case, and the Recent Publications of Professor Gibson.[2] In a real sense this pamphlet served to establish MacGregor's reputation as a theologian of no mean ability. Whilst not denying in any way total depravity affecting all man's faculties, MacGregor did hold that this did not mean that man was not capable of rational and even in some senses elevated thought and action. MacGregor distinguished "natural" from "spiritual" knowledge. In this way, in a sense, he makes an argument for what became later more commonly known as "common grace" – an expression that does not appear in the Westminster Standards, but which can be argued is implicit in them. In relation to the image of God in man, although certainly lost in the sense of involving the right exercise of *spiritual* or *moral* faculties, MacGregor argues that none-the-less man has not lost all faculties distinguishing him as a man as created by God, especially in the power of reason and having a sense of the divine. This, essentially, is what he means by "Natural Theology." The Professor held that the students had given too much place to the power of man's faculties in the understanding of divine truth. He saw what he considered to be incipient Pelagianism, namely, that man's will is not so impaired that he is incapable of some good. It is true that the *Confession* teaches that "The light of nature sheweth that there is a God."[3] There must then be some natural propensity to see this, at the very least. It is undeniable that unregenerate men are capable of many fine works. Yet care must be taken to affirm that by nature man is

---

[2] Edinburgh, 1859. This pamphlet of 80 pages was issued in a second edition the same year.
[3] *Westminster Confession of Faith*, XXI:I.

not capable of any *spiritual* good. After all, by nature people are "dead in trespasses and sins" (Ephesians 2:1) and in need of regeneration; of being "made new" (2 Corinthians 5:17). As long as a Church maintains the true gospel and strong evangelicalism it may be that this "natural theology" will not encourage distorted views of man's native ability in relation to the things of God. But man has a propensity to think of himself as well able to grasp truth by virtue of his natural intellect or wisdom. Such notions will prove fatal for a Church.

In retrospect it may be said that the "rationalism" of such nineteenth century divines as James MacGregor, conceded too much to the "natural man," and was altogether too optimistic about the good of which man was capable without grace. That, however, is being wise after the event. In the end the Assembly of 1859 found that there was nothing in the position of the students, raised by Dr Gibson, to cause the Church alarm. At least Professor Gibson later graciously acknowledged that MacGregor's work in this matter had persuaded him of his acquaintance with the theology of the Reformation, such that he felt free to support his subsequent advancement to the Professoriate in New College.[4]

Barely twenty years after the Disruption the Free Church was overtaken by an issue which threatened to tear it apart. This concerned a proposed Union with another main-line

---

[4] *PDGAFCS*, May 1868, 215. The subsequent evident weakening of historic Calvinism in the Free Church arguably lends some credence to Professor Gibson's contentions in this controversy. Cf.: "When [R. S.] Candlish died in 1873 Disruption Calvinism was also on its death-bed." (Andrew L Drummond & James Bulloch, *The Church in late Victorian Scotland 1874-1900*, Edinburgh, 1978, 290).

Scottish Presbyterian denomination, the United Presbyterian Church. The United Presbyterian Church had arisen in 1847 from a Union of two Secession groups, the 'Relief Church' and the United Associate Synod of the Secession Church. These Secession groups had all arisen from splits from the Church of Scotland the previous century. A distinctive tenet of the United Presbyterian Church was what was known as 'Voluntarism.' Voluntarism is the theory in Church/State relations that it is not competent to the Christian ruler to exercise his authority and influence on behalf of religion in any form. It denied the rightness of the establishment in the nation of true Christian religion and the support of it by the State authorities. This was not the position of the Free Church, which very distinctly maintained the opposite theory, namely, the Establishment Principle, or in other words the responsibility of the State authorities to maintain true Christian faith working in 'partnership' with the Christian Church, yet not usurping authority over it in spiritual or solely ecclesiastical matters. In the early stages of talks between the relevant Committees of these Churches after 1863, when discussions began, no great agitation or disquiet arose. However, when it became clear in 1867 that there were some in the Free Church who would be quite happy to treat the Establishment Principle as an open question in order to promote not only closer links, but Church Union, there was a strong reaction within the Free Church, especially amongst those of a more conservative outlook.

When serious talks were opened up between the Free Church and the United Presbyterian Church in 1863 there was initially very little dissention about this, until it appeared that there was a distinct determination on the part of some to go beyond mere co-operation, and take the process down the road of Church union. That alarmed many within the Free Church. After all there were *prima facie* differences between the Churches on a whole range of issues, not least the matter of attitudes to National Christianity.

James MacGregor, like most in the Free Church, was initially not opposed to talks with the United Presbyterians. After all, they represented part of the Evangelical family, as distinct from the Moderatism to be found in the bulk of the Established Church. He was even prepared to believe the Churches were essentially of one mind. However, in an address in Paisley to mark the twentieth anniversary of the Disruption, he made a comment on the "contemplated union" which indicated that, if it were shown that there were significant differences between the Churches, then it would be better if there was no union. In his address on *The Headship of Christ* he wrote this: "With the ridicule and scorn with which some have spoken of 'points' of difference, as hindrances to union, I do not sympathise. A conscientious difference on a very small point may really be fatal to union, may render incorporation a hopeless impossibility, aye and until the difference disappear." He provides an effective illustration: "A, B, C, and D, are set, with their horses and ploughs to plough a field. The ploughing would be most thoroughly accomplished if they would all unite, harness their horses to one plough. But they conscientiously differ in opinion on the question, in what direction the plough should be drawn. A thinks it should be drawn only from East to West; B, that it should be drawn only from West to East; C is no less decided for drawing only straight South, and D for drawing straight North. They will all confess that the 'point' of difference is comparatively a small one. But if the difference be *conscientious*, so that each of them must and shall draw only in his own chosen direction, it is obviously best that each should work with his own plough in his own corner of the field; for if they should all attempt to work with one plough, there may be much drawing, but there will be little ploughing." His point? "*Suppose* that the Reformed Presbyterian Church differs from the Free and U.P. on the comparatively small 'point' of one term of membership in full communion; that she feels constrained in conscience to admit no man to her membership unless he profess to believe in the descending obligation of the Covenants; while the larger bodies cannot in conscience allow any one to be excluded from church-membership in any congregation under their charge *merely* because he does not believe in that obligation. Or *suppose*, again, that the U.P. Church differs from the Free and R.P. on the 'point' of one term of office; that she feels constrained in conscience to allow her office-bearers to *deny*, if they will, the doctrine of national responsibility to God; while the two other bodies feel constrained in conscience to make this doctrine a part of their public testimony, by requiring the profession of it as a term of office. However small the 'points' may be in themselves, yet a conscientious difference regarding them, *affecting, as they do, the ordinary public action of the Church as a whole*, would be obviously fatal to incorporation, would lead to an inevitable dead-lock, and end in a disastrous failure." What would the responsibilities of the Churches be in that case? MacGregor concludes that "if there be any such conscientious difference, between churches really one, in prevalent spirit and fundamental doctrines, it is their duty to work and pray for a removal of the difference by a more full common understanding of God's word; and in the meantime, walking up to what they have attained, to exercise and evidence their real unity of spirit and truth, by outwardly uniting in reciprocal good offices of brotherly love, and, so far as practicable and wise, by co-operation in such work as home and foreign missions, the education of youth, and the training of ministers."[5]

It was clear, then, that there were certain problems in relation to union from inherent differences – on the face of it – between the two Churches. The United Presbyterians were 'Voluntaries,' and the Free Church maintained the 'Establishment Principle.' These views were hardly compatible. It was clear by 1867, however, that many in the Free Church, some of them very influential characters, were prepared to leave that matter as an 'open question' in the Church in order to take forward union proposals. It was at that point – when the Union Committee in the Free Church maintained at the General Assembly that year that the matters of Church and State were "no bar" to Union that opposition to the Union became more vocal and more organised. But it was not just on the question of National Christianity that differences were considered to exist between the Churches. MacGregor himself, in one of the most brilliant contributions to the debate, drew attention to the contentious matter of the position of the United Presbyterians, or at least some of their most influential figures, on the question of the extent of the

---

[5] James MacGregor, *The Headship of Christ*, Edinburgh, 1864, 32.

Atonement. MacGregor was one of several Professors of the Church who came to oppose the Union. On that side were James Buchanan, John Duncan, James Gibson and George Smeaton, though the first three of these men were all called to their eternal rest before the matter was concluded.

In point of fact up to 1867 MacGregor consistently voted for the continuation of discussions and negotiations with the United Presbyterian Church. His mind was not settled as to whether the Churches were really of one mind sufficient for union or otherwise. It was when he discerned a distinct pro-Union agenda on the part of the Union Committee that he raised serious reservations. He finally broke a lance on the matter in 1870. In one pamphlet he states the issue, as he saw it, with great clarity: "No union can lawfully be formed where the reality of that requisite amount of unity has not been conclusively evidenced. This has been assumed in all the relative proceedings all through the last seven years, and appears from the nature of the case. All the Churches, all through the seven years' labour of enquiry about unity, have proceeded on the assumption that no new Union can be formed consistently with due regard to principle, except on the ground of an ascertained agreement of the Churches regarding all those principles which ought to be conserved in and by the constitution of the united Church. And this assumption of theirs is well founded in Christian truth and law. We are not permitted by Christ's law, we are forbidden by Christ's law, to enter into any Union at the cost of principle which ought to be conserved." What is the implication of this thinking? It is surely this: "The question, therefore, with reference to any project of Union is, for us, Does it manifestly conserve all the principles which ought to be conserved? And to this question, in relation to the project of Union on our table, I answer – No; we have not conclusive evidence of the reality of the requisite amount of unity."[6] MacGregor therefore had aligned himself with the "Anti-Unionists." He had done so on the basis of a range of issues, including a degree of incompatibility on the matter of Christ's Headship over the Nations, what he called "Dissenterism" which he saw as conflicting with thorough Presbyterianism on several points, with worship,[7] and, specially, the doctrine of grace in relation to the Atonement. But it was the matter of the presence, as he saw it, of Amyraldism in the United Presbyterian Church that he took up at length and in which he made his most effective contribution.[8]

MacGregor's conviction that there was a problem on the question of the Atonement arose from a controversy within the Secession Churches in the 1840s.[9] He saw the issue as being one of Amyraldism. Amyraldism (or Amyraldianism) had arisen in France out of the teachings of one Moise Amyraldus, or Amyraut, (1596-1664) of Saumur, who reacted to the position of the Canons of Dordt (1618-19) on the question of the divine decrees in relation to the Atoning work

---

[6] *Professor MacGregor's Speech: including a Reply to Criticism on his Pamphlet on the Question of Principle now raised in the Free Church; specially with reference to the Atonement*, Edinburgh, [1870], 13.

[7] The United Presbyterians had already adopted human hymns and permitted instrumental accompaniment in public worship services.

[8] James MacGregor, *The Question of Principle now raised in the Free Church specially regarding the Atonement*, Edinburgh, 1870, 41-76.

[9] For a discussion of this issue see Ian Hamilton's recent study: *The Erosion of Calvinist Orthodoxy. Drifting from the Truth in Confessional Scottish Churches*, Fearn, Ross-shire, [2]2010.

of Christ. In terms of the decrees of God Amyraldians maintained that consequent upon the permission of the Fall, God decreed the gift of His Son to render the salvation of all men possible. Seeing that man did not have the moral ability to believe savingly in Christ, by another decree God determined to give *special* grace to a certain number – the elect – to secure their salvation. By this understanding the Amyraldians were able to maintain, as they believed, the consistency of the universal gospel call to all without discrimination, with the limited application or destination to the elect only. In their view of things it could therefore be said to the sinner, "Christ has died for you and desires to save you." The problem was that the death of Christ for all, in their scheme, was "hypothetical." The Amyraldian could not say that Christ's atoning death actually secured the salvation of any, something, clearly, that undermined its efficacy and therefore devalued its purpose. "The notion of any substitution of Christ," argued MacGregor, "that does not infallibly secure by purchase the salvation of all for whom He died, is deeply dishonouring to the person and work of the adorable Substitute."[10] Furthermore, implying as it does changeableness in the divine decrees, these views must undermine the believer's assurance, "for that assurance is ultimately founded on the truth, that all God's purposes are unchanging and effectual, and that no sinner can ever perish for whom Christ gave His life in the cross. The assurance, therefore, is fatally undermined by the notion, that there *is* a changeable or ineffectual purpose of God, and that many of those for whom Christ gave His life shall nevertheless fall into

[10] ibid., 55.

death eternal."[11] The Amyraldian scheme, argued MacGregor, did not really deal effectively with the issue of the harmony of particular election and the universal gospel call. He put it this way: "Your notion, of a general purpose of God (as distinguished from that special purpose about which you and I are agreed), permits you, you tell me, to say to every sinner, 'God loves *thee*, or intends or desires to save thee.' But at the same time it binds you, if you will be in this matter an honest man, to go on to say, further:– '*Yet*, I cannot tell whether He loves thee *so as* to secure thy salvation, or *so that*, once knowing that He loves thee, thou shalt know at the same time that thy salvation is infallibly secure. For aught that I can tell thee, regarding what I call His love to thee, He may have sovereignly ordained thee to thy deserved doom of everlasting death.'

"Your notion, again, of a general substitution of Christ in His death (as distinguished from that special substitution regarding which you and I are agreed), enables you, you tell me, to say to every sinner, 'Christ died for *thee*.' But at the same time it binds you in Christian honour to add:- 'Nevertheless, I cannot tell thee whether He has or has not really redeemed thy soul from death. If thou believe not now, thou art under condemnation now:– the clouds of God's wrath brood over thee unremoved; the lightning curses of His law pursue thee through life; and, though Christ have in some sense died for thee, yet, for aught that I can tell, He may, even in dying, have been purposely leaving thee to death eternal.'"[12]

---

[11] ibid., 55.
[12] ibid., 56.

How, then, does the Calvinism of the "old school" address this matter of the free offer of the gospel in the context of election and particular redemption? MacGregor put it beautifully: "I cannot tell thee whether God loves thee as He loves His own, nor whether Christ has died for thee, as He surely has died for all the elect: that can be known by men only when Christ lives in thee, and thou lovest God and man. Nor can I explain to thee *how* the free invitation of the gracious gospel to all may be harmonized with the sovereign particularism of grace in election and redemption. There is a mystery here too vast for my narrow and shallow comprehension. Here I have nothing to draw with, and the well is deep. But this I can tell thee, for this is what God has told me in His word:– His love, with which He loves His own, is freely offered to thee as thy life. The all-sufficient fullness of His Christ is freely offered to thee as a 'way' to life in His love. The bosom of that love which is life is wide open to thee as the sky. The arms of that love are stretched out far to thee from the cross. The voice of that love cries, Come, to thee, in the Spirit, through the Bride. And if only thou hear, thy soul shall live. Only give thyself over, a lost sinner, into the arms and bosom of that freely-offered love, and that love of God shall be thy portion, and the righteousness of Christ shall be thy white raiment, and the Spirit of Christ shall be thy new and true life, and thou shalt be saved, for ever and ever."[13]

In his pamphlet MacGregor effectively expounded the "old school" Calvinistic view of the sincere or *bona fide* or genuine gospel offer by way of an 'aside':

---

[13] ibid., 56-57.

(1) *As to the Gospel Offer and Call*, MacGregor maintained that the Calvinism of the old school did not seek to explain how a sincere invitation to all men may be harmonised with the doctrine or fact of the election and redemption of only some. He used the analogy of the sincere address of the Ten Commandments to all, though God gives the ability to keep them only to some. So, in relation to the gospel call, "the old school men, though confessedly unable to give a *rationale* or explanation of the fact, yet affirm the fact itself, that God sincerely invites all sinners to believe and be saved."[14]

(2) *In relation to the disposition of God*, MacGregor maintained that there is a "Divine complacency in man's well being and well-doing."[15] Whilst maintaining that there is no such thing in God as a saving purpose, intention, or desire, that does not infallibly determine salvation, the old school nonetheless held that there is in God a "certain complacency or delight in man's holiness and happiness; such that He is really pleased when men obey His law, and really displeased when they obey not." And MacGregor went as far as to say this: "He sincerely mourns over the misery of the unbelieving impenitent as lost, while sincerely rejoicing over the blessedness of the penitent believers as saved."[16]

(3) *As to aspects of redemption that Christ's death achieved*, MacGregor again affirmed that there is no substitution or suretyship of Christ but for the elect. Nevertheless, old school Calvinists maintained that God's redeeming grace had certain

[14] ibid., 50.
[15] ibid., 51.
[16] ibid., 51.

implications for all men indiscriminately. MacGregor mentioned three things:

(a) God's redeeming grace in Christ secures for all a season of suspended judgement and of offered mercy;

(b) It provides, further, a fullness of saving merit, amply sufficient for the salvation of all; and

(c) the Atoning sacrifice gives an open way by which God comes with free salvation to man, and men are freely invited to go for that free salvation to God.[17]

In dealing with the all-sufficiency of grace, MacGregor denied that it is the basis for the offer in the sense of constituting a *warrant* to sinners to appropriate Christ, or ministers in their invitations to sinners. "The fact of there being abundant provision in a certain house does not warrant a hungry stranger in entering and feasting." "That abundance," he maintained, "can of itself serve only as a *motive* to enter, or *encouragement* to enter."[18] What serves as a *warrant* then? "The only thing that can really serve as a true warrant is an invitation or permission from the owner of the house."[19] "In like manner, we say, the all-sufficiency of grace in Christ does not of itself constitute a true warrant to us, who 'were afar off,' in taking Him and His riches of grace to ourselves. Our only true warrant in this act of faith, is the permission or invitation of God in His Word."[20]

In applying this all to the question of relations with the United Presbyterians, MacGregor, in his understanding of the

---

[17] ibid., 51-52.
[18] ibid., 52.
[19] ibid., 53.
[20] ibid., 53.

position of the United Presbyterian Church in relation to the extent of the Atonement, maintained that "there is some reason to suppose that Amyraldism, or un-Calvinistic universalism, with reference to the Atonement, is *tolerated* in her pulpit by the United Presbyterian Church."[21] On the other hand, MacGregor wrote, "there is much reason to believe that Amyraldism is excluded from the pulpit of the Free Church by her law; or, in other words, that it is condemned, expressly and directly, by the Westminster Confession."[22]

MacGregor, therefore, was not convinced that the Churches were sufficiently of one mind on the question of the Atonement, and on that account, apart from other evident differences between the Churches, he could not see his way to support the moves for union between the Free and United Presbyterian Churches.[23] "I am persuaded," he was to say in another pamphlet, "that a Union in the manner now proposed, without any further, any real, ascertainment of the mind of the Churches, would involve the united Church in that calamity and sin, of looseness or indefiniteness in adherence to ostensible terms of office, in relation to the supremely great Christian doctrine of the atonement."[24]

In the event the crisis in the Free Church over this issue of proposed union with the United Presbyterians was averted at the 1872 Assembly when the leaders of the majority pro-union party dropped the proposals for incorporating union in the

---

[21] ibid., 59.
[22] ibid., 60.
[23] ibid., 75.
[24] *Professor MacGregor's Speech: including a Reply to Criticisms of His Pamphlet on the Question of Principle now raised in the Free Church; specially with reference to the Atonement*, Edinburgh, [1870?], 47.

interests of maintaining a unity, such as it might be, within the Free Church ranks. However, proposals for a Mutual Eligibility scheme by which United Presbyterian ministers might be called to Free Church Congregations (and *vice versa*) was brought forward into the 1873 General Assembly. This approach was supported by James MacGregor, on the grounds that only those UP ministers who were entirely at one with the Free Church constitutional position would come in to the Free Church, whereas those who were happier with the UP position would move from the Free Church to the United Presbyterians. To him it was an ideal solution.[25] This was typical of MacGregor's independent spirit. Most of the Anti-Unionists, however, saw these moves as union by the back door. It was strenuously opposed in the 1873 Assembly in view of the fact that the 'Mutual Eligibility' was not specifically on the basis of accepting the Free Church Formula of 1846 *including its Preamble*. As a result of a conference in between times among some of the leaders of the pro-union party, Robert S. Candlish, in one of his last acts in a General Assembly, came back in the evening with a modified motion in which to a large extent the concerns of the anti-unionists were met. That modification saved the day as far as a split was concerned, but William Nixon, George Smeaton and many other ministers and elders recorded their dissent on the basis that (1) the deliverance contained an unqualified approval of the Reports of the Committee on Union; (2) the declaration relative to the Headship of Christ over nations was inadequate; and (3) because the Mutual Eligibility Overture

---

[25] See his letters on the subject as printed in pamphlet, *The Union Committee's New Proposal*, Edinburgh, 1872.

was made the permanent law of the Church. In all 132 ministers and elders dissented from the decision of the Assembly on the matter of Mutual Eligibility, out of a total of around 600 Commissioners.

As far as the Free Church was concerned, this was the last involvement James MacGregor had on the matter of Church union. His name is, however, connected with an ecumenical venture which came to fruition in the formation of the *General Presbyterian Council*, – later the World Presbyterian Alliance. This Council was first convened at Edinburgh in July 1877. In May 1868 MacGregor had written a piece on "Our Presbyterian Empire" for the periodical *The Presbyterian*. In the article he advocated the desirability of "holding a Council of Presbyterians who hold by the Presbyterian Standards, once in five, ten, or twenty years, alternately at Edinburgh, London, and New York." The purpose envisaged was that "all the Churches might confer for oecumenical purposes, while each Church, for local purposes, would always retain her own autonomy, and hold herself perfectly free to accept or reject the decisions of the Council in the exercise of her own independent judgement under Christ."[26] The body held 19 Councils up to 1970 when there was a union with the International Congregational Council. This union produced the theologically diffuse *World Alliance of Reformed Churches*, the

---

[26] W. G. Blaikie, "Introductory Narrative," to *Report of Proceedings of the First General Presbyterian Council convened at Edinburgh, July 1877*, Edinburgh, 1877, 2. William Garden Blaikie (1820-1899) was Professor of Apologetics and Pastoral Theology in the New College (1868-1897) and Convener of the General Committee of the Presbyterian Council, 1875-1877. He became first President of what became known as the World Presbyterian Alliance, 1888-1892. See also John T. McNeill, *The History and Character of Calvinism*, New York, 1967 [1954], 387.

liberal position of which was very different from MacGregor's original vision.[27]

---

[27] For a history of the World Presbyterian Alliance and its successor, see Donald K. McKim (Editor), *Encyclopedia of the Reformed Faith*, Edinburgh, 1992, 403-407.

6

MACGREGOR'S MEMORIAL

Prior to the middle of the nineteenth century the predominant materials used in sung praise in the Presbyterian Church in Scotland were the Psalms, especially the *1650 Metrical Psalter*. After 1781 there was a limited use of Paraphrases in some congregations of the Church of Scotland, but the sanction given to the *Scottish Paraphrases* that year was temporary and never actually became the law of the Church. The use exclusively of Biblical materials of praise arose from the principle enshrined in the *Westminster Confession of Faith* (1647):

> ...the acceptable way of worshipping the true God is instituted by Himself, and so limited to His own revealed will, that He may not be worshipped according to the imaginations and devices of men, or the suggestions of Satan, under any visible representation, or any other way not prescribed in the holy Scripture.[1]

The Formula that office-bearers subscribed was also perfectly clear. They vowed to "own the purity of worship presently authorised and practised in the Free Church of Scotland," which practice was accepted as being "founded on the Word of God, and agreeable thereto." The said office bearer promises to assert, maintain and defend the said worship and

---

[1] Chapter 21, section 1.

follow no divisive course from it.[2]

Things changed in the Presbyterian Churches in Scotland in the nineteenth century. Discussions took place in the Free Church from the mid eighteen sixties about "expanding" the praise materials beyond the Metrical Psalms. A Committee on Paraphrases and Hymns was appointed in 1866 under the Convenership, initially, of the Rev. Robert Buchanan (Glasgow) and in 1869 it reported to the General Assembly favourably to the introduction of "human hymns."[3] James MacGregor was a member of this Committee and he was not happy with the arguments and conclusions of the *Report*. However, at that time he was Convener of another Church Committee – the Church and Manse Committee – and was prevented from taking his full part in the deliberations of the Committee on Paraphrases and Hymns. When it became clear that he had serious reservations about the draft *Report* going up to the May 1869 General Assembly, MacGregor sought to submit his statement of objections on it to the Committee *in absentia*. The draft *Report* had been sent to him in April and he found it so strongly objectionable that he "could not, with a safe conscience, allow it to pass to the Assembly with a silence on his part equivalent to constructive consent." He therefore sent a statement of his objections with a letter to the Convener (Dr John Adam at that time) through Dr James Begg, a fellow-member of the Committee. He requested that "if his objections should not be sustained as against the

---

[2] See Rev. Robert Forbes, *Digest of Rules and Procedure in the Inferior Courts of the Free Church of Scotland*, Edinburgh, [4]1886, 168-169.
[3] On this issue see the author's *Sing the Lord's Song! Biblical Psalms in Worship*, published by Crown and Covenant Publications, Pittsburgh, Pennsylvania, [2]2003.

Report, he requested that they should be recorded and transmitted as his reasons of dissent from the adoption of the Report." Apparently, the statement was not so much as allowed to be read. "The Committee refused to listen to the objections of a member of the Committee, presented in the only way practicable for him." To exonerate his conscience MacGregor subsequently produced a "Memorial" on the subject which he remitted to the 1869 General Assembly.[4] This at least revealed the sort of processes resorted to in pushing through such changes in the Church in those days, and, it has to be said, the implicit shift in the perception of the sufficiency of Scripture in the matter of praise materials in public worship.

What was the problem that MacGregor, and others too, had with the Hymns issue? Essentially it was the matter of *principle* over the introduction into worship services of songs or materials not given by inspiration of God. What were his particular objections? The *Report* made certain *explanations* as to the nature and effect of the proposed expansion of praise materials to include non-inspired items. One of these was that it was only permissive and not mandatory. MacGregor objected to this. To his mind that was not a fact. If passed, the proposal would inevitably be intrusive. It would permit, for example, the majority of a congregation to intrude hymns on a conscientious minority, or a minister/probationer on a conscientious congregation. "Even to 'permit' what is wrong can never be right; and my difficulty is that I cannot see that

---

[4] This detail is from James MacGregor's preamble to his 'Memorial,' as found in *PDGAFCS*, Assembly Papers, May 1869, 152. The entire Memorial is found in pages 152 to 161 in these Papers under 'Cases.'

the measure is not wrong in its principle." It was also said that
the hymns would be of unexceptionable quality and limited in
number. It seemed obvious to MacGregor, though, that no
matter how excellent a hymn may be in the right place, it
cannot be right to intrude it in the wrong place! To the same
effect, in relation to quantity, "if the intrusion be *in its nature*
illegitimate, then to speak of the 'limitation' of the *amount* of
intrusion is really worse than idle."

The *Report* also made statements in *justification* of the
proposals. The first of these was that the proposal to
"enlarge" the praise materials to include uninspired hymns
would be agreeable to the feelings and judgement of so many
respected brethren in the Church. This may be so, answered
MacGregor, but it cannot possibly be a determining reason for
adopting such radical legislation. He considered this "a species
of ecclesiastical corruption." The feelings of men, however
well respected, are not the issue, but the teaching of the Word
of the Lord is, and the feelings and judgements of men must
be brought into line with the Word.

The second statement he took issue with was the notion
that the measure to introduce such hymns was "*in harmony with
the hitherto practice of our Church.*" Apart from the fact that even
previous practice required to be brought into line, or be
deduced from, the teaching of the Word of the Lord, this was
arguably a serious misrepresentation of the case. How so?
MacGregor wrote that,

(1) there was a question as to whether the Church had really
ever given full and careful consideration to the *principle* in
connection with appropriate materials for praise in the
Church. If so, no real weight should be placed on what may

be thought to be the position in the past. In any case, wrote MacGregor:

(2) "The Report not only ignores, but in effect obliquely denies, that which is the leading characteristic fact of our Church history in the present connection – the fact, viz., that our Church, for many generations, has not, in her congregational praise, made any use of materials of merely human inspiration; and that, with reference even to materials of divine inspiration, the ambiguous *quasi*-sanction attained by the 'paraphrases' dates only from a very recent period in her history, derives its origin from the deepest darkness of her 'dark age' of moderatism." In the third place,

(3) the Committee seemed to lend some credibility to their arguments in favour of the hymns with reference to five such items normally included at the back of Psalmodies along with the Paraphrases. But these MacGregor characterised as "partly Socinian, mainly deistical, wholly unevangelical at heart." To him they seemed simply to be dragged in from the fly-leaves of the psalm books to give some foundation to the acceptance of *any* hymns. This was another case of historical misrepresentation in the *Report*.

The third statement MacGregor objected to is the argument that went this way: that in the Word of God they could see nothing that directly or indirectly "fettered" Christian liberty in the praise, any more than in preaching or prayer. This has been an oft-used argument from the hymn-singing side. James MacGregor, however, brought several strong objections to bear on this argument. He found it especially offensive. Why? For one thing, the phrase about "fettering Christian liberty" has to him a far from Christian ring. Because the impression is given that if God's Word *was* found to forbid man-inspired hymns, this would be seen from God's side to be a fettering of *our* "Christian liberty." But such an idea is really consistent with the perverse notion that to be bound to God's Word is to be in bondage. It is always in joyful conformity to all God's Word that true liberty lies, and there cannot be any fettering of man in that. Again, the *Report* seemed to be arguing that the Committee could see no prohibition to the use of non-inspired hymns. To this, MacGregor could see several objections:

(1) This was in effect the loose principle of the Ritualistic Churches, namely, that everything is lawful which God has not *forbidden* in His Word. The high and strict principle of the Reformation Churches is that everything is unlawful which God has not *prescribed or permitted* in His Word. The position of the *Report*, therefore, falls away from the principle attained hitherto, that "the absence of prescription and permission will be to us an effective prohibition."

(2) The point may be made, in addition, that the question is not what we may think we "see" (or do not see) in the Bible, but what really is in the Bible? MacGregor observed the following: "In the first place, the Bible gives us a God-inspired 'Book of Psalms.' In the second place, if the materials in that book do not suffice, in our new dispensation, for the utterance of congregational praise, yet we have additional materials, abundantly sufficient, in other parts of the Bible.[5]

---

[5] It is not entirely clear to what MacGregor is referring here. It may be that he is thinking of Scripture Paraphrases. Although such songs would constitute divinely inspired materials, we would take issue with the use of such compositions in public worship on the following grounds: "(1) *There is no clear warrant in Scripture for putting into verse for singing parts of the Bible not*

And in the third place, in the whole Bible record there is not one case in which we 'can see' that, with the sanction of God, any congregation ever made use, in its praise to Him, of any materials not given by His inspiration."

(3) There is then the question of the analogy with prayer and preaching to consider. On this MacGregor believed that the comparison of praise with prayer and preaching merits the *opposite* conclusion to the one given in the *Report*. How so? Well, for one thing, because if they really be parallel it would follow that if we have a *form* for hymns (from outside the canon of Scripture), then we should have *forms* for public preaching and praying, so that our public praying and preaching may be of a piece with our congregational song. For another thing, in any case the functions can in fact be contrasted. After all, 'free' prayer and preaching are possible in their nature, whereas 'free' praise is not possible because everyone has to sing from some source book all at the same time. Unlike prayer and preaching praise can thus *never* be 'free' in the sense *they* are or can be! In terms of *Scriptural warrant*, there is no evidence of a warrant for man-inspired song, though for 'free' prayer and preaching there is abundant warrant. In addition, there is a contrast among these exercises in terms of *Biblical provision*. Material for congregational praise is provided for. This is not the case with prayer or preaching,

---

originally recorded in the form of song, and (2) *it is rather presumptuous for any person or group of people to take upon themselves the responsibility for selecting passages to be adapted for singing*. After all, if the Lord has not caused such passages to be expressed in the form of songs nor indicated that such passages should be paraphrased for singing, by what authority do men take on this responsibility?" (John W. Keddie, *Sing the Lord's Song*, Pittsburgh, ²2003, 11).

albeit there are recorded prayers and sermons in Scripture (or at least parts thereof). Prayer and preaching will always be adapted to the changing circumstances of people's life experiences, whereas the praise materials relate to the God who is worshiped, who is the same, yesterday and today and forever.[6]

MacGregor's conclusion was that the "the Report is not fit for its purpose, to guide a Church in her Christian legislation, regarding a matter of vital importance to the spiritual life of her members." It is interesting to observe how the arguments deployed by James MacGregor are echoed in the *Minority Report* presented by Professor John Murray and Dr William Young to the General Assembly of the Orthodox Presbyterian Church in 1947. It is also notable that the Free Church Committee on Paraphrases and Hymns made no attempt to answer MacGregor's Memorial. One must conclude that they had (by a majority at least) *already* decided to go down the road of non-inspired hymnology, and as in other Presbyterian Churches, sound arguments against that position were not going to hinder the supposed 'advance' in that direction.[7] There was just a suggestion too that the Committee was not a

---

[6] The "Memorial" of Professor MacGregor was reprinted under the title *Professor MacGregor on Hymns*, in the, *The Watchword*, a periodical edited by James Begg, August 2, 1869, 210-215.

[7] It is of more than passing interest that in November 2010 the Free Church of Scotland, which had remained out of the union of the majority of the Free Church with the United Presbyterian Church in 1900 (which formed the United Free Church), yielded to the same species of arguments which had been used by the Committee in 1869 to overturn the position of the Disruption Church on worship. Such forms of worship had been restored and clearly reasserted in the post-1900 remnant Free Church in 1905 and 1910.

little influenced by the fact that there were union negotiations going on with the United Presbyterians who had already gone down the line of non-inspired hymns in their worship. This influence on the Free Church's practice in worship caused MacGregor some concern: "I therefore observe with grief and alarm a tendency in our own Church to be influenced in her judgement regarding this matter of internal administration by impulses naturally and, perhaps, inevitably proceeding from the more external movement about union."[8]

Whatever MacGregor's subsequent attitude to hymns and organs may have been, we cannot now say for sure. He must, however, have always entertained serious reservations about using any other materials in public praise than those materials given under divine inspiration. His concern was for the *principle* of the matter and on that question his "Memorial" was one of the most searching pieces of work to come out of the hymns controversy in the Free Church of the nineteenth century.

---

[8] James MacGregor, *The Question of Principle now raised in the Free Church specially regarding the Atonement*, Edinburgh, 1870, 22.

7

PROFESSOR IN NEW COLLEGE

With the retirement of James Buchanan (1804-1870) from the Chair of Systematic Theology in the New College at the end of the 1867/68 Session, a successor was required to be appointed by the 1868 General Assembly. Buchanan had been in that Chair for twenty years. He had authored many substantial works, several in the area of Christian Apologetics. However, his best-known works were *The Office and Work of the Holy Spirit* (1842), and his 1866 Cunningham Lectures on *The Doctrine of Justification*. Both these works have been reprinted in recent times. Of the latter James Packer, in an Introduction to a 1961 reprint of the work, was to say this: "It is doubtful whether a better exposition of it exists. And his preacher's style imparts a warmth to his writing which we do not find in (say) the lawyer-like Cunningham, and which is very refreshing. There is no doubt that this is still the best text-book on its subject, from the standpoint of the classic covenant theology, that the student can find."[1]

As we have indicated, James MacGregor himself acknowledged his indebtedness to Buchanan in influencing his own thinking on Systematic Theology. Little would he have thought, however, that he would have been considered as his

---

[1] J. I. Packer, Introductory Essay, in James Buchanan, *The Doctrine of Justification*, London, 1961, 9.

successor. It may be that his scholarly theological contributions to the *British and Foreign Evangelical Review*,[2] and his fine exposition of *The Sabbath Question* in 1866, together with the earlier Text Book on *Christian Doctrine* commended MacGregor as a worthy successor to Buchanan. Dr Robert Buchanan[3] – no relation to James Buchanan – put James MacGregor's name forward for the Chair in the General Assembly, on Friday, 29th May 1868. Among other things Buchanan states that the fact that MacGregor had been a minister for twelve years "in itself was a very important preparation for filling the Chair of Theology. He thought it was of the highest importance that a professor of divinity should have a thorough knowledge of what a minister's work was."[4] The motion of Dr Buchanan's was seconded by the outstanding layman, the Earl of Dalhousie. Proposed against MacGregor was the Rev. Marcus Dods,[5] even then a man known to be of somewhat broader sympathies. Supporting MacGregor's appointment was Dr James Gibson,[6] Professor of Systematic Theology in the Glasgow College, and a man of

[2] See the *Bibliography (A)* in pages 197ff. below.
[3] Robert Buchanan (1802-1875) was then minister of the College Church, Glasgow. He was the author of *The Ten Years' Conflict* produced in two volumes, 1857/1859.
[4] *PDGAFCA*, May 1868, 215. This was in the debate on Report XXVII, Report on the Election of Professors.
[5] Marcus Dods (1834-1909) was minister at Renfield Church, Glasgow (1864-1889) before his election to the Chair of Exegetical Theology in succession to George Smeaton in 1889. He was a man of liberal inclinations and took the Free Church along such lines in the latter part of the 19th Century.
[6] James Gibson (1799-1871) was a strong constitutionalist within the Free Church of his time. He was Professor of Systematic Theology in the Glasgow College from 1856 until his passing in 1871.

unquestioned orthodoxy. In view of the position MacGregor took against Gibson in the "Glasgow College Case" (1859) it may have been thought that he (Gibson) would have a prejudice against MacGregor. However, says Gibson: "It was in connection with that circumstance that I learned that Mr McGregor was thoroughly acquainted with the Theology of the Reformation, and that is no small matter in the present day."[7] In the event, when a vote was taken between MacGregor and Dods, the result was as follows:

"For Dr Buchanan's motion   263
For Dr [John] Adam's motion   175
Majority   88
Mr McGregor was accordingly declared to be elected."

It was said later that MacGregor had been "fortunate in being elevated at a comparatively early age to the important Edinburgh chair he occupied, and it must be owned that at the time of his election he had done very little to justify the choice. There was, however, the impression abroad of his great cleverness – an impression which he did not by any means belie."[8]

A letter survives which MacGregor wrote to John Stuart Blackie not long after he began the Professoriate in New College. He confesses to Blackie, who had invited him to some sort of a Greek Literary 'event,' that, "My professorial labours, of initiation, have left me in a condition, regarding Greek Literature, such that, among you, I would be as a beast of the field. I once told you, I think, that I have twice read the

---

[7] *PDGAFCS*, May 1868, 215.
[8] Obituary Notice in *The British Weekly*, Thursday, December 6th, 1894. No. 423 – Vol. XVII, 99.

body of Greek literature, from Homer to Demosthenes, and twice read the Latin Classics, from Placitus to Quintilian."[9] This at least gives a glimpse of the extent of MacGregor's learning as he took up the duties of his Chair at New College.

James MacGregor was inducted to the Chair on Thursday, 29th October 1868.[10] His first lecture in the Chair was subsequently printed under the title "The Competency of Theological System," basically a defence of the practice of Systematic Theology. He closed his lecture with this challenge: "…though that religion should suffice for your personal salvation when apprehended only in its 'beggarly elements,' yet in this form it will be comparatively 'weak' for the conquest of the world, or rather, for the great war of the world's liberation through the gospel. For this grand campaign, the true crusade, for which you are preparing, our religion will attain to its full power in you, not when its truths are in your mind as a confused rabble, without discipline or captains, but when they are marshalled in their due order, of facts under doctrines, and doctrines under principles, and *all under Christ*, shining on the world in magnificent array, 'Fair as the moon, clear as the sun, and terrible as an army with banners.'"[11] In 1871 Edinburgh University conferred on MacGregor the honorary degree of Doctor of Divinity.

---

[9] Letter of James MacGregor to John Stuart Blackie, 19th November 1869. *Blackie Papers*, MS 2629, National Library of Scotland Catalogue, Vol. II, Edinburgh, 1961.
[10] *The Watchword*, Volume III, December 1868, 346.
[11] James MacGregor, *The Competency of Theological System*. Lecture delivered on entering upon the duties of the chair [of Systematic Theology] in the New College, Edinburgh, 1868, 8.

As far as MacGregor's classes were concerned we have information in the Reports of the Committees or Commissions on the Quinquennial Visitations of the New College. In James MacGregor's time there were such visitations in 1871 and 1876. In the 1871 Visitation MacGregor mentions five elements of his work:

(1) Lectures in each class, three days a week.
(2) Oral examinations on the lectures, one day a week.
(3) Written examinations on lectures, and on the prescribed portions of classic works, Latin and English, about once in five weeks. Those who take Latin are not required to take the English.
(4) In junior division [first year class of Systematic Theology in the second year of a College course], I am entitled to call for a short essay, not oftener than once a month. The four best essays are read in the class, and the authors criticise one another's compositions. The professor reports on all.
(5) In both classes, the Fridays, as often as available, is devoted to notes on books and study.

There was a mixture in other words of lecturing and what we might call tutorials. There were two classes – second year students taking the first class, and third year students the second. By way of suggestions in 1871 MacGregor said this: "I should like to have as a fixture, some twenty copies of *Calvin's Institutes* and forty of *Cunningham's Historical Theology*. I find that perhaps about a third of the students would go with me, by written examination, through the first three books of Calvin, and the remainder, – excepting the non-effectives – through the relative portions of Cunningham."[12] This effectively shows

___

[12] *PDGAFCS*, May 1871. Report XXVII – Report of Commission on Quinquennial Visitation of the New College, 11.

MacGregor's perspective in his course work. It is clear, however, that MacGregor developed a great liking for the *Systematic Theology* of Charles Hodge which was completed in 1873.[13] It is evident that he used Hodge's 3-volume work in New College, after 1874.[14] MacGregor was a Calvinist of the Old School, however independent a line he may have taken on issues arising in the Church. A contemporary scholar said of MacGregor that he was "trained in the school of the strong, logical theology of a former age, and gifted with a vigorous intellect, he was equalled by few either in acquaintance with the great system-builders of the seventeenth century, or in the power of handling difficult dogmatic questions."[15]

There is little added in the 1876 Visitation Report, although MacGregor does imply that his suggestions of five years earlier had been more or less attended to satisfactorily. He does, significantly, add one thing: "In the lectures I habitually call attention to 'the rhetoric of Inspiration,' or the place which this and that matter occupies in the manifested mind of God, and the way in which it is brought by the Spirit home to the mind and heart of men."[16] There is perhaps more

---

[13] See his appreciation of Hodge's work in, "Dr Charles Hodge and the Princeton School," *The British and Foreign Evangelical Review*, July 1874, 456ff.

[14] Cuthbert Lennox, *Henry Drummond*, London, 1901, 19.

[15] S. D. F. Salmond, in, *The Critical Review*, Vol. 5, 1895, 83. *Stewart Salmond* (1838-1905) was Professor of Systematic Theology and New Testament Exegesis in the Free Church College in Aberdeen. His perspective was clearly broader than MacGregor's and less sympathetic with the classic Reformed Theology of the Westminster Standards.

[16] *PDGAFCS*, May 1876. Report XL – Report of Commission for Quinquennial Visitation of the New College, 14.

than a suggestion here that MacGregor was aware that the
question of the Inspiration of Holy Scripture was becoming
an issue for the Church.

As far as the impression made upon the students was
concerned, there is one interesting reference in the biography
of Donald John Martin by Norman C. Macfarlane. He wrote:
"Professor James MacGregor…was a Celt with deep strains of
genius and eccentricity. He was a thinker and a mystic, and
fond of deep waters. In theological speculation he was
disported. He re-appeared after a while's submergence, and
then with a soft plunge, as of a porpoise, went down again. He
was the soul of geniality. On one occasion he invited the
whole College to his classroom. He invited his brother-Celt,
the blind organ grinder of the mound, also to come. That lent
a breath of novelty. He had his sorrows that forced him to
lighter themes, and he read some of those light productions.
Greek, Gaelic and English tongues had their innings. The air
was full of interest."[17]

On his departure from the College James MacGregor
received 'testimonials' from former students. One of his
former students, Alexander Campbell Smith, was to write this
of his former teacher in a letter written from Rothesay on 19th
May, 1881:

> You always impressed me as being one who not
> merely knew theology, but a *theologian* who had
> found truth for himself, and made theology part of
> himself, as had almost no one whom I had ever
> met or heard speak. You always seemed to have a
> very wide grasp of Christian doctrine as a *whole*,

[17] Rev. Norman C. Macfarlane, *Rev. Donald John Martin*, Edinburgh, 1914, 34.

and to look at each part in the light of the whole. I, for one, had long been troubled by difficulties and doubts, and had found many things in our Calvinistic system hard to reconcile with each other. I found you solving the difficulty in a single luminous sentence. I think I am now a pretty sincere Calvinist. I do not think I would have been such had I not heard your lectures; for these helped me greatly to reconcile the system with a belief in God's love.[18]

---

[18] This may be seen in *The Pamphlet Collection of Sir Robert Stout, Volume 65*, on the web-site of the Victoria University of Wellington Library: http://nzetc.victoria.ac.nz/tm/scholarly/tei-Stout65-t21.html (accessed 27th March 2014).

8

THE ROBERTSON SMITH CASE *

Professor Thomas Smout in his *A Century of the Scottish People 1830-1950* highlights events in the Victorian period in Scotland which attracted widespread attention. He pinpoints the Disruption in the Church of Scotland in 1843 as one of these. From that 'Disruption' a significant number of ministers and people went out of the Established Church to form the Church of Scotland, Free. He goes on to say that "scarcely less marked was public interest in the trial of Robertson Smith for heresy by the Free Church in 1881."[1] The irony of the situation is that both these events involved the Free Church of Scotland, a denomination which was initially acknowledged for its strong evangelical and orthodox position. The rise of the critical movement in Biblical studies within its bounds indicated a serious shift in the position of the Church in respect of adherence to the inspiration and authority of Holy Scripture. That critical movement heralded a

---

* The substance of this chapter first appeared in *The Evangelical Quarterly*, Vol. XLVIII. No. 1, January-March 1976, 27-39, under the title "Professor MacGregor, Dr. Laidlaw and the Case of William Robertson Smith." It has been extensively reworked here.

[1] T. C. Smout, *A Century of the Scottish People 1830-1950*, London 1987, 181-182. In point of fact the conclusion of the 'Robertson Smith Case' was not a trial for heresy as there was no 'libel' pursued in the General Assembly in 1881. Smith was simply removed from his professorial chair that year essentially on grounds of expediency.

terrible declension and downgrade in the credibility and power
of the Church in the land. It is only fair to say that those who
initially embraced the critical positions in the Scottish Church
believed there was no inconsistency between those positions
and traditional evangelical faith. The truth was that it was an
indicator of a loss of evangelical faith, based as it had always
been on a high view of the inspiration, authority and historical
accuracy of the Bible. After the critics had done their work it
was clear that in the popular perception the basis of Christian
faith in an infallible record had been dealt a mortal blow. The
significance of the case of William Robertson Smith before
the courts of the Free Church between 1878 and 1881 cannot
be overestimated.

In this chapter we examine James MacGregor's position in
this watershed case in Biblical criticism. MacGregor was no
mean theologian. But what would he make of the issues
involving the Old Testament criticism propounded by his
erstwhile pupil, William Robertson Smith? If MacGregor had
a bit of the genius about him, he also had a bit of the erratic.
This is something that came out in frankly his odd position on
the matters raised by Smith.

On December 7, 1875, Volume III of the ninth edition of
the *Encyclopaedia Britannica* appeared. It included an entry under
the caption "Bible," contributed by the Professor of Hebrew
and Old Testament in the Free Church College, Aberdeen,
William Robertson Smith, then a young man of twenty-nine.
On March 3, 1876, alluding to some criticisms of the article
which had come to his ears, Professor James MacGregor, of
New College, Edinburgh, a former teacher of Smith's, wrote
to warn him that it might bring him some trial of his

"Christian wisdom and fortitude," adding: "I am thankful you have spoken out what *must* soon be said by some one, and what ought to be said first by our qualified experts in Old Testament study."[2]

The attitude of James MacGregor in the Robertson Smith Case is of interest among other things on account of the fact that, as Smith's biographers put it, "…Professor MacGregor, as Professor of Dogmatic Theology, was perhaps entitled, and even bound, to have an opinion on the questions raised by Smith's article."[3] MacGregor's position receives little mention in the standard church histories and has received little, if any, attention even in those works that have been regarded as authorities on that case.[4] It is important to note that MacGregor adhered strongly to the *Westminster Confession of Faith* and was an advocate of the traditional views of revelation over against the higher critical theories and constructions.[5] William Brenton Greene, Jr, of Princeton wrote of MacGregor's later work, *The Apology of the Christian*

---

[2] J.S. Black and G. Chrystal, *The Life of William Robertson Smith*, London, 1912, 175-176.

[3] ibid., 186. The biographers are referring to the article "Bible" in the *Encyclopaedia Britannica*, 9th Edition, Volume III, 1875.

[4] See, for example, J. R. Fleming's *Church History of Scotland, 1875-1929* (1933); C. G. McCrie's *Confessions of the Church of Scotland* (1907); and the biographies of *James Begg* (T. Smith, 1888), *David Brown* (W. G. Blaikie, 1898), *Robert Rainy* (P. C. Simpson, 1909), and *Alexander Whyte* (G. F. Barbour, 1923). Notable exceptions are Norman L. Walker's *Chapters from the History of the Free Church of Scotland* (1895), and of course Black and Chrystal's biography of *Robertson Smith* (1912).

[5] See MacGregor's *Studies in the History of Christian Apologetics*, Edinburgh, 1894, 238ff. See also H. D. McDonald, *Theories of Revelation*, London, 1963, 271-273. As regards MacGregor's orthodoxy see Professor S. D. F. Salmond, *Critical Review*, V, 1895, 83, and *British Weekly*, 423, XVII (1894), 99.

Religion, Edinburgh, 1891, that it was "written in the spirit of strong, I had almost said bitter, and yet most intelligent opposition to the Higher Criticism."[6] The issue had to do with the apparent acceptance within the Free Church of current theories about the origin and development of the religion and documentation of the Bible, especially in relation to the Old Testament. Such ideas were designated the "Higher Criticism," or, more narrowly, the "Documentary Hypothesis." The young Free Church Professor in Aberdeen, William Robertson Smith, clearly espoused these views in articles submitted to the 9th Edition of the *Encyclopaedia Britannica*, from 1875. The question was: how would the Free Church react to the challenge of his adopted position?

In a useful biographical *Memoir* by Professor H. R. Mackintosh of Professor John Laidlaw (1832-1906), MacGregor's successor in the Systematic Theology chair in New College, prefixed to a posthumous volume of Laidlaw's sermons there is reference to the case of Professor William Robertson Smith that throws light on the position taken in that case by James MacGregor.[7] We know from references to the case in MacGregor's own writings that it was he who was responsible for writing the motion which was presented to the Free Church Assembly in 1880 by Laidlaw, then a minister in

---

[6] *The Presbyterian and Reformed Review*, Vol. V, 1894, 110.

[7] H. R. Mackintosh, 'Introductory Memoir', prefixed to John Laidlaw, *Studies in the Parables*, London, 1907, 1-47. John Laidlaw (1832-1906) in 1880 was minister of the West Church in Aberdeen. In 1881 he was appointed successor to James MacGregor in the Chair of Systematic Theology in New College. Mackintosh (1870-1936) succeeded Laidlaw in the Chair of Systematic Theology at New College, upon the latter's resignation in 1904. See Hugh Watt, *New College, Edinburgh*, Edinburgh, 1946, 230-231.

Aberdeen, and which, with modification, did not differ greatly from the motion of the Rev. Alex. Beith (Stirling) which ultimately carried in the Smith case that year.[8] Basically, Laidlaw's motion, as originally framed by MacGregor, declared that "the views promulgated by Professor Smith to be not those of the Free Church, but inasmuch as they do not directly contradict the doctrine of the Confession, replacing him in his chair with an admonition."[9] MacGregor had earlier commentated that, "...these positions...do not directly affect any matter of Christian faith as confessed by our Churches...They do not...directly collide with any doctrine ever affirmed by any Christian Church in the world."[10] Beith's motion, not dissimilar to Laidlaw's, additionally contained a censure of Smith "on account of offensiveness in his *manner* of dealing with Holy Scripture."[11] Before dealing with the position of John Laidlaw and James MacGregor it is necessary

[8] MacGregor, *Freedom in the Truth*, Dunedin, 1890, 20-21. Cf. MacGregor, *Studies in the History of Christian Apologetics*, Edinburgh, 1894, 338; Mackintosh, op. cit., 32: "Dr. Laidlaw...made the proposal which was backed by Professor James MacGregor in a powerful speech ..." (cf. also page 34); *Proceedings and Debates of the General Assembly of the Free Church of Scotland* (hereafter, *PDGAFCS*), Edinburgh, 1880, 187-189 (speech of Dr Laidlaw); 189-193 (speech of Professor MacGregor); and Norman L. Walker, *Chapters from the History of the Free Church of Scotland*, Edinburgh, 1895, 282-284. See also J. S. Black and G. Chrystal, *The Life of William Robertson Smith*, London, 1912, 352.
[9] Walker, op. cit., 282-283.
[10] *Daily Review*, Thursday, July 20, 1876, Letter from "Presbyter": (Professor Smith's Article 'Bible'). For the identification of MacGregor as "Presbyter" see Black and Chrystal, op. cit., 186, and George Macaulay's *"Presbyter's" Defence of Robertson Smith Examined*, Edinburgh, 1876. Regarding the sentiments expressed see *PDGAFCS*, 1880, 187.
[11] MacGregor, *Studies in the History etc.*, p. 338. For the complete text of Beith's motion see *PDGAFCS*, 1880, 243-244. See also Walker, op. cit., 283.

to give some background detail on this crucial case, which first arose within the Free Church in 1876.

A reputedly brilliant theological student, William Robertson Smith (1846-1894), within weeks of his having completed the normal course of training for the ministry at New College, Edinburgh, was appointed to the Chair of Hebrew and Old Testament Exegesis in the Free Church College, Aberdeen by the Free Assembly of 1870. It was not long, however, before it became apparent "that the advanced views which had become current in Germany and Holland were affecting his own opinions as to the history and character of the Bible."[12]

Matters came to a head in 1876 after the appearance of an article by him entitled "Bible" in the 9th edition of the *Encyclopaedia Britannica*, published in December 1875. It was clear from the article that Smith's views of the literary structure of the Old Testament had been profoundly influenced by the continental advocates of Old Testament historical criticism, Karl Graf (1815-1868), Abraham Kuenen (1828-1891), and Julius Wellhausen (1844-1918), especially the latter's. Professor Alec Cheyne of New College, Edinburgh, summarised Smith's views, as expressed in that article in the *Encyclopaedia Britannica*: "Smith's published article assumed that the Scripture narratives which we now possess are not the originals but later, edited versions of accounts dating from various periods in Jewish history. In particular, it contended that the 'Mosaic' legislation had first been promulgated, if not actually composed, during Israel's exile in Babylon (hundreds of years after Moses) and under the influence of the great

---

[12] ibid., 272.

eighth-century prophets: its attribution to Moses was not fraudulent, of course, but simply in accord with the recognised literary conventions of the age. The article also suggested that most of the psalms had not been written by David, eliminated much of the predictive element in the prophets, and denied authorship of the Gospels to the evangelists whose names they bear. In sum, it required no extraordinary insight to realise that Smith's picture of the Bible, and of the Old Testament in particular, deviated very considerably from that which had long held sway in Scotland."[13]

These views have been described as the *Development* or *Documentary Hypothesis*.[14] Their reconstructions and dating of Israel's history and literature were largely informed by naturalistic evolutionary principles and Hegelian philosophy.[15] It is of interest to note that Smith spent two periods of study in Germany – in 1867 and again in 1869. He was influenced there by men like Richard Rothe (1799-1867)(Bonn) and Albrecht Ritschl (1822-1899)(Gottingen). He was also profoundly influenced by the philosophy of Immanuel Kant

---

[13] A. C. Cheyne, *The Transforming of the Kirk*, Edinburgh, 1983, 47. For another useful summary of the views expressed by Smith see also C. G. McCrie, *Confessions of the Church of Scotland*, Edinburgh, 1907, 180ff.

[14] E. J. Young, *An Introduction to the Old Testament*, London, 1964, 136-138. This hypothesis has been otherwise popularly known as the Graf-Kuenen-Wellhausen hypothesis. For an able brief traditional conservative response to the theory see Young, 139-141 and O.T Allis, *The Five Books of Moses*, Philadelphia, 1964. In 1896 the Church of Scotland minister W. L. Baxter (Cameron, Fife) wrote an able refutation of Wellhausen's (and Smith's) work: *Sanctuary and Sacrifice: A Reply to Wellhausen*, London, 1896, xviii+511pp.

[15] ibid., 137.

(1724-1804).[16] The influence, too, of A. B. Davidson (1831-1902) Smith's Old Testament Professor in New College, must not be minimized. Smith called Davidson his "master" and it was with some justification that Macleod wrote: "Davidson's teaching...became the source of an alien infusion in Old Testament studies in Scotland. Robertson Smith caught the infection and spread the plague."[17]

The views of Smith, thus moulded by alien critical and philosophical principles, came with shocking suddenness to the attention of the Free Church of Scotland. At that time (1876) the Free Church would be considered theologically orthodox and conservative. In the event, then, "it need cause no surprise...that a violent commotion was produced when a professor wrote an article in which no reference was made to the supernatural origin of the Bible, and in which the composition of several books was dealt with in the very freest manner, as if they had been put together by the wit of man alone. With criticism of this sort the Church was entirely unacquainted...the blow fell without warning."[18] The content of the article "Bible" was first of all brought to the attention of the College Committee in 1876 and a report was submitted to the Assembly of 1877, affirming insufficient grounds for a charge of heresy against Smith, though some points were

---

[16] Ronald R. Nelson, "The Theological Development of the Young Robertson Smith," *The Evangelical Quarterly*, XLV, No. 2, April-June 1973, 88-96. For a penetrating Reformed evaluation of the place and significance of Kant for modern Protestantism see Cornelius Van Til, *The Reformed Pastor and Modern Thought*, Nutley, N.J., 1971, 106-131.

[17] John Macleod, op. cit., 288.

[18] Walker, op. cit., 272-273.

thought unsatisfactory, as for example the question of the historicity of Deuteronomy.[19]

Earlier in 1877 – in March – a Commission of Assembly had instructed the Aberdeen Presbytery to examine Smith's articles, invite his own explanation of them, and report back. In connection with some questions on the matter which certain Presbytery members wished to put to Smith but were disallowed, an appeal was made direct to the Assembly of 1877 from the Presbytery. And thus, both through the College Committee and the Aberdeen Presbytery the matter was suddenly brought before the Free Church Assembly of 1877. The decision of that Assembly on the case was merely to suspend Smith pending the completion of the investigation of the Aberdeen Presbytery. This decision aroused Smith, who indicated his wish that a libel be drawn up in order to necessitate *a judicial process*. The Assembly acceded to this and instructed the Aberdeen Presbytery to prepare a libel for heresy against Smith. The original libel comprised three general and eight specific charges. The former of these and seven of the latter, were in due time regarded as being *irrelevant*.[20] The libel therefore was eventually reduced to one

---

[19] Smith's article on 'Angels' in the same *Encyclopaedia* raised serious questions about his belief in angels in general, and the fallen angels in particular. Sadly, the only dissenting voices in the College Committee on that issue were George Smeaton and David Brown (see *PDGAFCS*, 1877. Report V. A. Special Report of the College Committee on Professor Smith's Article "Bible," 30 (Smeaton's Dissent), 39 (Brown's Dissent).) Brown, however, only focussed on the question of the matter of Smith's views on angels, whereas Smeaton also addressed the question of Smith's views of the Bible and revelation.

[20] "To find a charge 'relevant' is to find that, if *proved*, it would involve censure. In charges of immorality the 'proof' is a separate matter from the relevancy. But in a charge of heresy, separate proof is not needed, because

count only, namely, that Professor Smith held the opinion that Deuteronomy was not a *genuine* historical record, that it was of late date, and that it was written by someone who passed it off as being the work of Moses, which of course, it could not have been according to his arguments, or, in other words, that it involved deception on the part of the *actual* author.[21]

It was in 1879 that the amended libel finally came before the General Assembly of the Church and was served on Professor Smith. Smith thereafter made a spirited defence of his position, and after some objections on points of order and relevance, the matter was passed over to the following Assembly (1880), where the decision was taken to abandon the libel. That decision, however, did not conclude the case for, shortly after, another article by Smith, this time on "Hebrew Language and Literature," appeared in the *Encyclopaedia Britannica.* The contents of this new article were even more fitted to offend the conservative section of the Church, with the result that the matter was, inevitably, brought again to the attention of the Church and in the Assembly of 1881 the momentous decision was taken to remove Smith from his Chair on the grounds that it was no longer considered "safe or advantageous for the Church that Professor Smith should continue to teach in one of her

---

the matter dealt with is in the author's own writings. If it be found 'relevant,' or contrary to the standards, the case is finished." (W. G. Blaikie, *David Brown*, London, 1898, 205.)

[21] Walker, op. cit., 280, for a summary of the original charges and the text of the reduced libel. Cf. MacGregor, *Studies in the History of Christian Apologetics*, 337-338.

Colleges" to quote the conclusion of the motion of Principal Robert Rainy (1826-1906) which was finally carried.[22]

It should be understood that Smith was *not* deposed for heresy for there was no libel – it had been dropped the previous year – neither did he forfeit his status as a minister of the Church, though he afterwards never did take a charge in the Church, nor accept a stipend.[23] He was removed from the Chair on the ground that he had lost the confidence of the Church. In other words, it amounted to merely a no-confidence vote. Subsequently Smith accepted the post of Lord Almoner's Readership in Arabic at Cambridge, becoming in turn a Fellow of Christ's College, University Librarian, and ultimately Professor of Arabic. For the rest of his short life he was more or less a closeted scholar. He died of tuberculosis in Cambridge in 1894 at the comparatively early age of forty-seven. Like his mentor, A. B. Davidson, he was unmarried. Neither of these men ever held a pastoral charge in the Church.

In the Assembly deliberations of 1880 on the libel process four motions were tabled. Those of Alexander Beith (1799-1891) and John Laidlaw have been briefly summarized above. Of the other two motions, one proposed by Sir Henry Wellwood Moncrieff (1809-1883) maintained that as Smith had in large measure forfeited the confidence of the Church, his Chair should be declared vacant. This was similar to the motion of Robert Rainy, which was carried the following year

---

[22] See *PDGAFCS*, 1881, 77, for the complete text of Rainy's motion. See also Walker, op. cit., 288-289.
[23] James MacGregor, *Freedom in the Truth*, Dunedin, 1889, 20; W. G. Blaikie, *David Brown*, London, 1898, 207.

when the matter was concluded. The other motion, by James Begg (1808-1883) – a man of decidedly conservative views – had urged the Assembly to proceed directly to prove the libel. Over against these positions, Laidlaw and MacGregor maintained that, as Smith could not be censured for, or charged with, any deviation from the Confessional *doctrine* of the Church, as they believed, the libel should be passed from, though not without (1) an admonition of Smith to exercise caution and desist from teaching the critical views; and (2) a declaration that his views were not those of the Free Church.[24] Against the first motion (Moncrieff's) Laidlaw objected that, whilst it was true that, abstractly speaking, the Church had a right to set aside office-bearers on the grounds that they had lost the confidence of the Church, "he denied that this procedure was appropriate in a case where a *Judicial process had already been entered on*."[25] That would only serve to "shed a lurid light on the peculiar precariousness of the tenure of office enjoyed by the professors. It suggested a discipline so flexible as to be seriously unworthy."[26] On the other hand, against Begg's motion Laidlaw objected that it might end in a verdict of "not proven" and, as he strongly disapproved of Smith's views, he feared, not without justification that any such result would mean that these views "might correctly be described as having triumphantly survived a judicial process."[27] Laidlaw

---

[24] Cf. Walker, op. cit, 286; *PDGAFCS*, 1880, 187. The motion of Laidlaw only received 51 votes in the division, against 244 for Beith's (*PDGAFCS*, 1880, 243).

[25] Mackintosh, op. cit., 32 (emphasis mine – J.K.); cf. *PDGAFCS*, 1880, 187.

[26] ibid, 32; *PDGAFCS*, 1880, 188.

[27] ibid, 33; *PDGAFCS*, 1880, 188.

clearly thought that *either* to condemn Smith by a narrow majority, *or* to remove him from his chair on the grounds that he had merely lost the confidence of the Church, would not carry much weight in the Christian Church at large. Furthermore, even more serious in his opinion was the fact that "views which he thought dangerous and rashly assumed would thereby only receive wider currency."[28] This is an important consideration in Laidlaw's line of argument for he felt that "if they deprived Professor Smith of his chair *after* libel, still more if they deprived him *after dropping* the libel, they would not stamp out his views."[29] If, on the other hand, he was sent back to his Professoriate with a declaration that his views were not acquiesced in by the Church, and enjoined to avoid matters of higher criticism and "imaginary literary hypotheses," there was a possibility that those matters would be relegated to the subordinate place they deserved.[30]

Clearly Laidlaw and MacGregor hoped that the views espoused by Smith would be refuted in due time, though they felt that, far from being achieved by a libel action or any such disciplinary process, such a process would probably give greater currency to the views. No doubt as long as they felt that an assurance was obtained along the lines they suggested, then these opinions could be left without danger to subsequent study, which would, they believed, show them up for what they were: "imaginary." In hindsight it is clear that this conviction, not uncommon amongst people thought to be

---

[28] ibid, 33, *PDGAFCS*, 1880, 188.
[29] ibid, 33; *PDGAFCS*, 1880, 188.
[30] ibid, 33; *PDGAFCS*, 1880, 189.

conservatives at that time, was naively sanguine, as subsequent history demonstrated.

How can we evaluate this case, and in particular James MacGregor's role in it? The following observations may be made:

(1) As to the *ecclesiastical process* in the case itself, it would seem that the libel as originally framed was not clear enough in showing how Smith's views really deviated from the Confessional doctrine of Scripture. It is arguable that if, as suggested by Walker,[31] a more direct indictment had been framed in the first place, such as: "You hold and teach a view of the Holy Scriptures which impugns and discredits the same as the supreme authoritative and infallible Word of God written and the inerrant source of religious truth," libel might have been proved. However, one must appreciate the extent to which the views expounded by Smith had *already* gained currency within the Free Church of Scotland through Smith's teacher A. B. Davidson (1831-1902), who as assistant to John "Rabbi" Duncan had been first Lecturer and Tutor and then Professor, of Old Testament at New College from 1858. There had been a 'strange silence' about Davidson's views in the Church. It is true that Principal John Macleod states that "Dr. Duncan, when his junior colleague, A. B. Davidson, began to show signs of going off on rationalistic lines…called in the help of [George] Smeaton to do what he could to reclaim him."[32] Davidson's position, however, was less explicit

---

[31] Walker, op. cit., 290-291. This form is a slight adaptation of the one suggested by Walker.
[32] Macleod, op. cit., 288: From where Macleod gleaned this anecdote is unattributed. There is no reference to such a situation either in the

and more cautious than that of the Continental critics, and it seems that he was of a more diffident disposition than his somewhat rash and impetuous student. In a real sense this made Davidson even more dangerous than Smith in loosening attachment to traditional and orthodox views of Revelation and Inspiration. To the end of his days Davidson never really reconciled his generally orthodox *theological* position with his *critical* views. Geerhardus Vos of Princeton Theological Seminary was to say this in a contemporary observation on Davidson's position: "One gains the impression that Dr. Davidson's views in regard to the content of truth of the Old Testament were substantially worked out in a period previous to his aligning himself with the modern hypothesis. Afterward the critical conclusions were superimposed, but they did not have time materially to reshape the body of doctrinal convictions"[33] It may easily be imagined therefore, that it would be all the more difficult *to prove* inconsistency between Confessional *doctrine* and the critical positions. Unfortunately, this was one of the 'knots' which tied up James MacGregor – and the Free Church – in the Robertson Smith Case.

(2) The case was undoubtedly complicated by Smith's strong claims of adherence to the *Westminster Confession* and Reformation principles. The use of evangelical terminology by such men in expressing their views served to impress many orthodox conservative theologians such as MacGregor. MacGregor himself was to say that, "It is perhaps a good

---

Biography of Davidson (J. Strahan, 1917) or Robertson Smith (J. S. Black and G. Chrystal, 1912).

[33] Geerhardus Vos, in a review of A. B. Davidson's *Theology of the Old Testament*, 1904, in *The Princeton Theological Review*, Vol. IV, 1906, 119.

thing that the positions have been maintained among us by a
Christian teacher so earnest and pronounced in his evangelism
as Professor Smith."[34] Later in his life he was to repeat the
same thing: "He [Smith]…was earnestly in sympathy with the
Church's evangelical faith."[35] As a result a basic dualism was
evident. Writing fifty years later Donald Maclean succinctly
outlined this position: "A frank dualism is proposed in which
a man can be a 'traditionalist' and a 'modernist' at the same
time by the use of evangelical phraseology connoting entirely
different conceptions from what a modernist actually believes.
In this way they shall *appear* to hold evangelical beliefs while
accepting modernist critical views."[36] In the realm of Biblical
scholarship this has bedevilled the Church over the years since
the days of the Robertson Smith Case.

With special reference to the Robertson Smith case,
Thomas Carlyle apparently exposed the futility of attempting
to maintain such a dualistic position when he said: "Have my
countrymen's heads become turnips when they think they can
hold the premises of German unbelief and draw the
conclusions of Scottish evangelical orthodoxy?"[37] It is possible
that Robertson Smith – and James MacGregor and others –
did not recognize the incongruity, or incompatibility, of these
views with the view of the Bible maintained by the *Confession of
Faith*. It seemed that there was a lack of awareness of the alien

---

[34] *Daily Review*, Thursday, 20th July, 1876.
[35] James MacGregor, *Freedom in the Truth*, Dunedin, 1889, 20. Cf. Blaikie,
op. cit., 198; and A. R. Vidler, *The Church in an Age of Revolution*, Penguin
Books, 1961, 171: "He [Smith] was an earnest evangelical who accepted
the Calvinist doctrines of the Westminster Confession."
[36] D. Maclean, *Aspects of Scottish Church History*, Edinburgh, 1927, 170-171.
[37] ibid., 171.

presuppositions under-girding Smith's work, or at least their logical outworking. Ronald Nelson, writing in 1973, brought this out when he wrote that "though Smith claimed the authority of the Protestant reformers for his position it is clearly evident that he was profoundly influenced by currents of thought flowing in the wake of the Kantian revolution. Smith's conversion to Neo-Protestant theology was the preparation for, not a consequence of, an acceptance of the correctness of the particular higher critical assertions about the Bible that he was to popularise in Great Britain."[38] Clearly there was not sufficient awareness by many at that time, including orthodox theologians like James MacGregor and John Laidlaw, of the underlying unbelieving principles and presuppositions in Smith's position, and *their* inconsistency with truly Protestant and reformed principles. It was not sufficiently discerned how devastating the promotion of such ideas would be to the spiritual health of the Church and Nation in the twentieth century.

(3) Though there is more than an element of truth in the view of Laidlaw and MacGregor that a non-proven libel or a vote of no-confidence, would, or at least might, have the effect of giving further currency to the views of Smith, in retrospect this view may be seen as a selling of the cause of truth down the river. After all, it would provide as wide an entrance for such views as their advocates may have wished.[39] Indeed, this was Smith's own reaction to the decision of the 1880 Assembly, which was not substantially different from Laidlaw's motion, and was used by him as the main thrust of

---

[38] Nelson, op. cit., 99.
[39] Cf. Macleod, op. cit. 308.

his defence of his subsequent article, "Hebrew Language and Literature."[40] It may be noted here that even the final Assembly decision of 1881, relieving Smith from the Chair in Aberdeen was considered by many of his friends as a triumph for his views.[41] However, in all fairness it must be pointed out that in the heat of the moment this position of Laidlaw and MacGregor must have seemed viable. After all, in the first place the case was unique, as MacGregor himself pointed out: "But that case, the like of which had not occurred once before in 300 years..."[42] In the second place Smith strongly professed his adherence to evangelical truth, including the inspiration of Scripture though, as pointed out above, it is a moot point whether what he meant by that term corresponded to the real position of the Westminster divines and the Reformed Churches. In the third place, it appears to have been their hope that future investigation would expose the groundlessness of the critical positions and, so to speak, bury them forever. MacGregor himself, with characteristic vigour and polemical bite, assails the critical positions in his later works on Apologetics, especially in his *Studies in the History of Christian Apologetics* in which he took much the same ground on the Old Testament question as William Henry Green and Geerhardus Vos of Princeton Theological Seminary. At one point MacGregor gives this withering critique of Robertson Smith: "The Cambridge Arabic professor is found to be in his thinking receptive rather than originative, – taking his philosophy from Herbert Spencer, his social archaeology from

---

[40] Walker, op. cit., 285-286.
[41] Vidler, op. cit., 173; Black and Chrystal, op. cit., 446ff.
[42] MacGregor, *Freedom in the Truth*, 21.

J. F. Maclennan, and his biblical criticism from the Continental school represented by Wellhausen. And in the mind so constituted and furnished there are found the same traits of unfitness for veritable criticism (=judgement) as elsewhere are found in that master, – rash arbitrariness in assumptions even as to fact, ignorance or ignoring of information outside of the 'cave' of a one-sided book-learning, and manifested incapacity for simply independent judgement on the ground of relevant evidence."[43]

In more recent times the Old Testament scholar O. T. Allis pointed out how there was real optimism amongst conservative scholars at the beginning of the twentieth century over the publication of James Orr's *The Problem of the Old Testament* (1906), which, it was hoped, would settle for ever the critical arguments surrounding the Old Testament.[44] It need hardly be said that this optimism was not realised. In retrospect there seems to have been considerable naivety on the part of such optimists. It may also be pointed out, that just four years earlier, in 1902, Orr took a similar position to MacGregor in a case before the United Free Church Assembly involving the advanced critical views of Professor George Adam Smith of the Glasgow United Free Church College. This Smith was another former pupil of Davidson. He had entered the Free Church ministry a year after the conclusion of the Robertson Smith case.[45]

---

[43] MacGregor, *Studies in the History of Christian Apologetics*, 269.
[44] O. T. Allis, *The Old Testament, its Claims and Critics*, Nutley, N.J., 1972, vii; cf. Young, op. cit., 139.
[45] See J. R. Fleming, *The Church in Scotland 1875-1929*, Edinburgh, 1933, 59.

In a recent scholarly book advocating Biblical inerrancy, and therefore critical of 'modern and postmodern' approaches to Scripture, one contributor wrote that "The nineteenth-century source-critical consensus has completely collapsed in the past thirty years, and today there is little agreement about anything. Consequently, Rolf Rendrorff could recently write, 'The Wellhausen paradigm no longer functions as a commonly accepted presupposition for Old Testament exegesis.'" This is a striking irony when one thinks of the impact of such views in the Scottish church, and elsewhere, in 19th century and the misplaced conviction that such views were really 'progressive' and somehow would advance the effective witness and credibility of the Church. This is not to say, sadly, that a rejection of the 'Wellhausen paradigm' has heralded a return to a conservative or traditional view of the Old Testament and its history and documents, but it does suggest a certain folly in going after the latest subjective theories, albeit in the name of 'advanced' or 'progressive' scholarship![46]

(4) Whilst at this distance in history one might be inclined to be somewhat cynical over what one may consider pious optimism on the part of these men (Laidlaw, MacGregor and Orr), this must be counter-balanced by the fact that *they* did not possess the historical perspective of later generations – the benefit of hindsight. The fact is, however, that able theologians and scholars of the calibre of MacGregor and Orr

---

[46] James K. Hoffmeier, "'These Things Happened': Why a Historical Exodus Is Essential for Theology," in James K. Hoffmeier and Dennis R. Magary (Editors), *Do Historical Matters Matter to Faith?* Wheaton, Illinois, 2012, 108.

should have discerned more clearly that the *logical outcome* of the basically naturalistic positions espoused by Robertson Smith *et al* would be modernism…and worse. In his monogram on *Freud* Rousas J. Rushdoony has a comment on the impact of Robertson Smith on the Social Sciences: "The anthropology he [Sigmund Freud (1856-1939)] went to, moreover, was ostensibly religious but actually naturalistic, namely, William Robertson Smith's (1846-1894), whose works, in particular *The Religion of the Semites*, are basic to an understanding both of the meaning of modernism in the churches and of Freudianism as a psychology."[47]

(5) It is scarcely tenable to maintain, as MacGregor and Laidlaw did, that no *doctrine* of the *Confession of Faith* was impugned by the critical positions.[48] There is a real dichotomy between the *Westminster Confession's* doctrine of the inspiration of Scripture involving the *supernatural* origin of the Bible, the canon of Scripture, etc. and the doctrine of the critics, naturalistic, evolutionary, and modernistic as it was. Far from being not contradictory, these positions are really diametrically opposed. As R. L. Dabney aptly commented: "No fair man doubts but that the *Confession of the Free Church*, Chap. 1, sec. 2, means to assert what Mr. Smith distinctly impugned touching

---

[47] R. J. Rushdoony, *Freud* (Modern Thinkers Series), Philadelphia, 1965, 21. See also page 24 of that work. The work of Robertson Smith in question was *Lectures on the Religion of the Semites. Fundamental Institutions. First Series* (London: Adam & Charles Black 1889); second edition, edited by J. S. Black (1894).

[48] See *Westminster Confession of Faith*, Chapter One. Cf. Hugh Martin, *The Westminster Doctrine of the Inspiration of Holy Scripture*, Edinburgh, [3]1877, for a contemporary discussion of that matter from the conservative side. See also B. B. Warfield, *The Westminster Assembly and Its Work*, Cherry Hill, N.J., 1972, especially 261-333.

the Old Testament canon. It is no new thing, indeed, in church history, to find the advocates of latitudinarian views raising this false issue"[49] But this was something other Free Church divines also discerned. George Smeaton, for example, dissented from the original report of the special sub-Committee set up in 1876 in these terms: "I hold that the doctrine of Inspiration and Professor Smith's views are irreconcilable."[50] As Nelson put it: "Smith emphatically rejected...prepositional revelation, an infallible Bible, and a static system of doctrine."[51] Such 'rejections' could hardly be claimed of the compilers of the *Westminster Confession*! John Macleod later stated that "In his later years [Smith]...came to see...that his attitude to Holy Scripture was quite out of harmony with the Westminster Confession."[52]

(6) It is arguable that, as Smith alleged, in the Scottish Reformed tradition there was too much reliance upon *systematic theology* at the expense of *biblical theology, antiquities and exegesis*. Smith maintained – as Davidson had done before him[53] – that there was an inclination within that tradition to inform the exegesis by a pre-supposed dogmatic system.[54] Of course Robertson Smith went far beyond simply an

---

[49] R. L. Dabney, *Discussions: Evangelical and Theological*, London, 1967, Vol. I, 401.
[50] *PDGAFCS*, May 1877. Report V. Appendix IV, 34.
[51] Nelson, op. cit., 99.
[52] Macleod, op. cit., 310. The source of this comment is not provided by Macleod.
[53] A. B. Davidson, *A Commentary on the Book of Job*, Vol. I, London, 1862, vi: "We in this country have been not unaccustomed to begin at the other end, creating Exegesis and Grammar by deduction from Dogmatic, instead of discovering Dogmatic by induction from Grammar."
[54] Nelson, op. cit., 97-98.

examination of 'Biblical Theology' in his work. He adopted speculative notions and applied evolutionary principles to his understanding of the Old Testament history. Exegesis and literary or historical analysis, however, will inevitably be influenced by presuppositions and such studies require to be guided by truly biblical and theistic presuppositions. Absolute neutrality is not possible.

Be that as it may, to some extent this may explain why, when the Robertson Smith case came to the forefront, there was general inability in the Church to deal conclusively with the matters raised. It may also help to explain why there was a tendency towards a dualistic position – the separation of dogmatics and the work of biblical criticism – that is to say, the assumption that the critical conclusions did not or could not subvert the theology, so that James MacGregor could make this strange schizoid statement: "The cluster of propositions maintained by the professor…are in their nature not theological, but archaeological. They refer, properly, not to matters of Christian faith, but to matters of biblical antiquity…Supposing that the Bible is the divine record of the divine revelation, any further question about the way and manner and purpose of the origination of detailed portions of the record is theologically unimportant."[55] Later on MacGregor was to defend his position thus: "All through the history of his [Smith's] case…I constantly took his part, on the view that his critical opinions…might be held, sincerely though mistakenly, by one believing, as he professed to believe, the Confessional Westminster doctrine of the

---

[55] *Daily Review*, Thursday, July 20, 1876.

inspiration of Scripture."[56] MacGregor, however, ought to have seen that "William Robertson Smith...sought to accomplish the impossible task of reconciling the newer views of Wellhausen...with the doctrine of inspiration stated in the first chapter of the Westminster Confession of Faith."[57] It would seem clear that inadequate views of the *nature* of the Bible inevitably distort views of the *content* (i.e. doctrine or history), as subsequent history has demonstrated. A theologian and thinker of the stature of James MacGregor ought to have discerned this. He did not see the warning lights.

(7) As far as adherence to the *Westminster Confession* was concerned, it is perhaps ironical that MacGregor was in fact generally unsympathetic with modifications. In a later pamphlet he was to write this about the teaching of the *Confession*: "...there is nothing in this whole complexity of detailed articulations that occasions perplexity where men are agreed upon the substance of the whole: the Calvinism, in straight-forward clear simplicity, is 'all in the whole, and all in every part'; so that a real Calvinist in going to this and that detail, finds only a cause for satisfaction on account of the masterly manner in which the substance of doctrine believed by him is here worked out into the detailed application."[58] "We are greatly favoured," he says further, "by possessing in it what, in respect of strongly guarding the Christian doctrine which it clearly and fully declares, is reputedly the best

[56] MacGregor, *Studies in the History of Christian Apologetics*, Edinburgh, 1894, 335.
[57] E. J. Young, *Thy Word is Truth*, London, 1963, 194.
[58] James MacGregor, *Presbyterians on Trial by Their Principles*, Dunedin, 1890, 29.

constructed of all the great historical creeds."[59] It has to be said, however, that MacGregor and other conservative men like him, did not sufficiently discern the real divergence between the views of the *Westminster Confession* on the matter of the inspiration of Scripture and those of the critical school, especially on the *nature* of biblical revelation and inspiration.

There were those in the Free Church at those times who were clearly alarmed by the tendencies in historical criticism. George Smeaton (1814-1889), for example, was not only an outstanding exegete and Biblical theologian and scholar, he was also clear on the issues involved in the Higher Criticism. He had been at New College as Professor of Exegetical Theology since 1857 and was the author of immense books on the Atonement. He had studied these matters exhaustively. As early as the first College Committee Report of 1877 he entered his explicit dissents. He was aware that it was said that the negative criticism (i.e. so called 'Higher Criticism') could be separated from the underlying philosophy. He was not convinced, however, that they could be sundered. Whilst in one generation there may be acceptance of a certain inter-weaving of supernatural elements, how could one have confidence that future generations would not yield to the basic anti-supernatural philosophy behind the sort of criticism proposed? And then the question arose about the impact of all this on the doctrine of the inspiration of the Scripture? "Not only so," says Smeaton, "opinions which are fatal to inspiration, dislocating the unity of Scripture, and undermining the canonical rank of several books of Scripture on petty grounds of internal criticism, can only be called

---

[59] ibid., 29-30.

dangerous error tending to heresy."[60] He for one maintained that the Church should have proceeded to a libel immediately, as we have seen. He wrote with reference to the tendency of the Higher Critical views: "An attack on the genuineness and authority of the Scripture, whether dignified by the title of the higher criticism or prompted by the lower scepticism, ought never to be permitted within the Church on the part of any office-bearer. We can keep criticism within its proper limits, and this occasion may have been permitted to occur that we may show to other churches how we can act in the exercise of our independent jurisdiction."[61] Besides Smeaton there were other Free Church men who wrote able books against the critical positions, such as Alexander Moody Stuart (1809-1898)[62] and George C. M. Douglas (1826-1904), the Professor of Old Testament Language and Literature in the Glasgow Free Church College.[63]

MacGregor's inconsistency on the matter of Robertson Smith and his critical views really arose from two arguably unsatisfactory positions:

(1) First of all there was his failure to recognise that the critical views essentially challenged the confessional doctrine of Scripture, because they challenged the reliability of the Bible as a faithful historical record. He was taken in by the claims of those favourable to the historical criticism both in relation to

---

[60] *PDGAFCS*, May 1877. Report V. Appendix IV, 32.

[61] ibid., 37.

[62] A. Moody Stuart, *The Bible True to Itself: A Treatise on the Historical Truth of the Old Testament*, London, 1884.

[63] G. C. M. Douglas, *Why I still believe that Moses wrote Deuteronomy*, Edinburgh, 1878; G. C. M. Douglas, *The Old Testament and its Critics*, Glasgow, 1892.

the inspiration of the Scriptures, and in relation to the evangelical doctrines of the *Westminster Confession*. As a result, he failed to appreciate the differences there were in the use of terms in both these areas: inspiration of Scripture and evangelical doctrine and experience. It didn't seem to strike MacGregor that the 'believing critics' (as he would have seen it) adopted the exact same presuppositions held by the unbelieving or 'destructive' critics, and just how much at odds these presuppositions were with the confessional view of the Bible as to its nature and inspiration.

(2) Secondly there was his feeling that the critical matters needed to be aired to avoid an undue interest being generated in the issues if they were simply suppressed. He did not agree with the views but he clearly miscalculated just how settled and influential the critics were, even in the Free Church, on the critical positions, not least through the work of A. B. Davidson over many years. He also miscalculated how difficult they would be to counter effectively if they were tolerated for the purpose of debate, albeit not accepted formally in the Church. Decisive action was required but MacGregor was not inclined to be decisive in outlawing the views in the Church.

This was a naïve position. It was exposed by fellow Free Church minister James Smith of Tarland, Aberdeenshire. Smith, commenting on an article of MacGregor's which had appeared in the *British and Foreign Evangelical Review* in April 1877,[64] wrote that: "Others also we find assuming awkward

---

[64] James MacGregor, "Age of the Pentateuch, with Special Reference to Revelation and Inspiration," *The British and Foreign Evangelical Review*, Vol. XXVI, No. C, April 1877, 254–274.

positions, which appear to us inconsistent, and which it must be impossible permanently to occupy. Professor Macgregor, e.g., considers the question about the Mosaic authorship of the Pentateuch as one 'not of abstruse scholarship, but of morality,' and that any one personating Moses would probably have been stoned as a profane person; he is strongly of opinion that Christ was completely committed to the Mosaic authorship, and he regards it as 'inconceivable that God should have inspired or authorised any man to put on the false face of the supposed impersonation.' But then again, he tells us that, if we insist upon all this, we run the risk of driving some men into infidelity! that we must not only permit but encourage the new teaching – no doubt, under the plausible guise of 'scholarly inquiry' – otherwise we will do 'enormous damage to the Christian cause in the rising generation'! If we ask, in alarm and amazement: How so? we are told that 'the question is exercising the minds of our young people, and must exercise it more and more until the question is definitively settled in the way of real ascertainment' – all which is a mere hallucination; our young people are not greatly exercised about anything of the kind. There is much exercise of another sort among others than our young people in the Church at present."[65]

---

[65] James Smith, *Professor Smith on the Bible*, Edinburgh, 1877, 44. Smith (1838-1900) was Free Church minister at Tarland, about thirty miles west of Aberdeen. Smith was closely involved with the case as it came before the Free Synod of Aberdeen in 1879. See his *Professor Smith's New Plea and the Presbytery's Procedure; Being the Substance of a Speech delivered in the Free Synod of Aberdeen, 14ᵗʰ October, 1879*, Edinburgh and Aberdeen, 1879. This is an able speech of 44 pages which was published by request.

It is only fair to say that there is no evidence that personally James MacGregor deviated from the traditional positions on the matters raised by the historical criticism of the Bible. In his later two-volume Handbook on *Exodus* (Edinburgh, 1889), and trilogy of Apologetic works (Edinburgh, 1891-1894), he takes up positions against the critical positions. In the Robertson Smith case, however, he showed himself to be inconsistent and undiscerning on the issues in question. He apparently said of his New College Colleague, George Smeaton, that he had "the best-constituted theological intellect in Christendom."[66] It is just a pity he did not follow his older colleague on this matter of the critical positions of Robertson Smith. Not that he accepted Smith's critical views – by no means. In his Assembly Speech of May 27th 1880 he went as far as to say this: "If I object to the new view and refuse to dismiss the professor who is said to hold it, what am I to do in favour of the received view which I embrace? Well, if life and health be given me, I may endeavour to refute the new views off the face of the earth."[67] It has to be said that this was something he attempted in his later works in Apologetics.[68] No lesser theologians than the Princeton divines, William B. Greene and Benjamin B. Warfield, thought highly of these volumes of MacGregor's.[69]

---

[66] John Macleod, op. cit., 289. Macleod, unfortunately, does not provide the source of this statement.

[67] *PDGAFCS*, May 1880, 191.

[68] *The Apology of the Christian Religion*, Edinburgh, 1891, 544pp; *The Revelation and the Record*, Edinburgh, 1893, xii+265pp; *Studies in the History of Christian Apologetics*, Edinburgh, 1894, ii+370pp.

[69] See Dr Kim Riddlebarger's 1997 Doctoral Dissertation, *The Lion of Princeton*. Benjamin Breckinridge Warfield: Apologist, Polemicist and Theologian. See pages 167, 180, 259, 284, 287, 296-7, 299, 351, 360 of the

It is clear from his last book, *Studies in the History of Christian Apologetics*, that MacGregor had a high regard for the work of the American conservative Old Testament scholars, including the Princeton Professors William Henry Green and Geerhardus Vos.[70] By that time, sadly, the critical views had prevailed in scholarly circles. As Alec Cheyne put it in 1980: "Long before 1914, the view taken by [W. R.] Smith, [J. S.] Candlish, [A. B.] Bruce, and [M.] Dods had triumphed in all the major Presbyterian Churches in Scotland, and the Biblical revolution had run its course."[71]

The effect of this 'revolution,' however, is another thing. The deadening effect on vital faith in the critics themselves, and the subsequent impact on the Church and true piety have rarely been examined. In relation to the last decade of the 19th Century in this connection Kenneth Ross commented that, "Given the force of the spreading naturalism of the late nineteenth century thought, the instinct of faith scarcely seems an adequate defence for the integrity of a supernatural religion. Yet it was the very strength and conviction of their evangelical faith which persuaded [Marcus] Dods and others that their Christianity was impregnable. It blinded them to the fact that the concessions they made broke down the orthodox

---

on-line edition (http://kimriddlebarger.squarespace.com/b-b-warfield-the-lion-of-pr/). This has subsequently been published under the title *The Lion of Princeton: B. B. Warfield as Apologist and Theologian* (Lexham Press, 2015).

[70] See, MacGregor, *Studies in the History of Christian Apologetics*, 279: "Professor Green of Princeton (*Moses and the Prophets*, etc.), protagonist there of the received Christian view in its completeness; whose judgement in a *real* of Old Testament Hebrew scholarship is perhaps the weightiest now in the Christian world." See page 279 and following for admiring remarks by MacGregor on American conservative scholars.

[71] A. C. Cheyne, op. cit., 57.

line of defence so that the essence of faith was exposed to serious danger. They never appreciated the magnitude of what was done in the 1889-1892 period."[72]

Exactly what the strength and conviction of the 'evangelical faith' of these men was must be debatable. In a revealing comment written in 1902, Marcus Dods (1834-1909), a Free Churchman who had embraced the newer criticism, surmised: "I wish I could live as a spectator through the next generation to see what they are going to make of things. There will be a grand turn up in matters theological, and the churches won't know themselves fifty years hence. It is to be hoped some little rag of faith may be left when all's done. For my own part I am sometimes entirely under water and see no sky at all."[73] The truth is that very little of a 'rag of faith' has survived in Scottish Church life. The legacy of the 'newer criticism' was far-reaching and destructive to the strength and conviction of evangelical faith, by which alone authentic Christianity can really prosper.

James MacGregor was conservative in his biblical and systematic theology.[74] It is passing strange, however, that he did not see that the critical views effectively undermined the authority and historical integrity of the doctrine and authority of Scripture which he himself maintained. More discerning was fellow Free churchman, Alexander Moody Stuart, whom

---

[72] K. R. Ross, *Church and Creed in Scotland*, Edinburgh, 1988, 222-223.

[73] *Later Letters of Marcus Dods, D.D.* (Selected and Edited by his son, Marcus Dods, M.A., Advocate), London, 1911, 67.

[74] More recently the historian, Peter C. Matheson, onetime Lecturer in Church History at New College, Edinburgh, stated that "McGregor was a considerable scholar of the old Calvinist mould, with a well-stocked, subtle mind." (Stewart J. Brown and George Newlands (eds.), *Scottish Christianity in the Modern World*, Edinburgh, 2000, 129.)

MacGregor cites with approbation in his *Studies in the History of Christian Apologetics*.[75] Moody Stuart in 1884 wrote perceptively on the issue of the critical views and their consequences: "The word of the Lord is pure, and out of this trial will come forth in all its brightness as silver out of the furnace. But, meanwhile, an unutterable calamity may overtake us, for our children may lose the one treasure we are bound to bequeath to them; and for long years they may wander 'through dry places seeking rest, and finding none,' before they recover their hold of the Word of Life, and regain their footing on the rock of eternal truth."[76]

James MacGregor himself recorded in a footnote to his last book on apologetics remarks made to him by Alexander Duff (1806-1878) about the critical views: "Dr. Duff, 'the prince of missionaries,' said to the present writer, in answer to the question, How the new critical views would work in India? that they would be simply ruinous, destroying the foundations."[77] What was true for India was also true elsewhere, as the history of the Church has subsequently indicated.

In the year of the conclusion to the case of William Robertson Smith (1881) James MacGregor, for reasons of his own health and that of his family, resigned his Chair at New College and emigrated from Scotland to New Zealand. The following year he took a charge at Oamaru in the South Island, within the Presbyterian Synod of Otago and Southland. He took his full part in the life of the Synod and

---

[75] MacGregor, *Studies in the History of Christian Apologetics*, 276.
[76] A Moody Stuart, *The Bible True to Itself*, London, 1884, 187.
[77] MacGregor, *Studies in the History of Christian Apologetics*, 309.

acquired a reputation as "in his time, the best-known Presbyterian theologian in Australasia."[78] Among other things he sought to counter the theologically liberal trends and the moves for confessional revision which were affecting the Churches in the antipodes every bit as much as in the old country. He was always active with his pen and frequently broke a lance in defence of traditional historic Calvinism.[79]

---

[78] Ian Breward, 'MacGregor, James,' from *the Dictionary of New Zealand Biography*, Te Ara – the Encyclopedia of New Zealand, updated 12-Nov-2013 (http://www.TeAra.govt.nz/en/biographies/2m8/macgregor-james, accessed 27 March 2014).

[79] See particularly his pamphlets: *The Day of Salvation (2 Cor. vi, 2) obscured in a recent pamphlet on 'The Reign of Grace.'* (Wellington and Dunedin: New Zealand Bible, Tract, and Book Depot, 1888); *Freedom in the Truth under Shield of a Constitution of Government and of Doctrine, in accordance with the Word of God.* (Wellington and Dunedin: New Zealand Bible, Tract, and Book Depot, 1889); and, *Blown in the Wind or Growing by the River? Presbyterians on Trial by their Principles.* (Wellington and Dunedin: New Zealand Bible, Tract, and Book Society, 1890).

9

THEOLOGICAL AND PRACTICAL WRITINGS

In the period of his Professorship James MacGregor was extremely busy with his pen.[1] As the century wore on the Churches were deluged by issues arising from both the physical and social sciences. As a consequence, tensions arose within the Churches, especially in relation to the authority of Scripture and, consequently, the matter of Creed subscription. There were movements for change from the old order. From the conservative evangelical perspective, the final quarter of the century was marked by declension in theological and biblical studies. Clearly, however, there were issues which were difficult to address, not least in the areas of Biblical Criticism, Darwinism, and social change in the wake of growing industrialisation and urbanisation. Pressures arose in the Church to accommodate to new ideas. In many areas there tended to be wholesale modification and even capitulation of conservative and traditional positions in the face of the

---

[1] In *Disruption and Diversity* (Edinburgh, 1996), the authoritative history of theological training in Edinburgh between 1846 and 1996, George Newlands in the chapter on 'Divinity and Dogmatics' comments that "James MacGregor appears to have written little" (p123). In reality Professor MacGregor was quite a prolific writer in his day, though it is true that no major books came from his pen in the time of his Professoriate. He did, however, produce a massive trilogy of volumes on Apologetics whilst in New Zealand.

onslaught, which arguably left a bitter legacy to the 20th Century of a Church greatly diminished in credibility and power.

James MacGregor was aware of the major issues. This is reflected in his writings. A feature of his writing in his period at New College was that he was not afraid to tackle crucial and controversial issues. For example, in the popular family paper, *The Christian Treasury* he contributed in 1872 two series of articles on Creation and Providence. More weighty were his contributions to such a prestigious periodical as *The British and Foreign Evangelical Review*, in which, especially in the late 1870s, he discussed such issues as the age of the Pentateuch, revision of the Westminster Confession, the doctrine of Creation, the Resurrection of Jesus, and the nature of divine inspiration, besides such practical, yet no less crucial matters, as the place of children in the Church.

His one minor book in this period was a modest *Handbook* on Paul's letter to the Galatians, which first appeared in 1879. This was the first in a projected series produced under the editorship, initially, of Alexander Whyte and Marcus Dods. On the whole the series was well-conceived and many of the volumes remained in print right up to the 1960s. The books produced were a mixture of Commentaries – or Bible studies – and historical or theological works. They were intended for "Bible Classes and Private Students," but they are rather more academic than popular. In perspective they tended to be a "mixed bag," though they were largely conservative. Some were first rate, such as William Binnie on *The Church* and John Laidlaw on *Foundation Truths of Scripture*. MacGregor's *Galatians* was the first of the Series. A brief volume of 127 pages, the

introduction and notes are sound and helpful. It seems that
the publisher, Messrs T. & T. Clark, tended to print sheets of
the volumes of this Series which were only bound as and
when required, a thousand at a time. In one notice of this
book of MacGregor's it is described as "Tenth Thousand."
The present writer actually obtained the last available bound
copy from the offices of T. & T. Clark, 38 George Street,
Edinburgh, in March 1968! MacGregor was later, from New
Zealand, to contribute a two-volume work on *Exodus* (1889)
in the same series. He also prepared a manuscript on
Immanuelism, the Doctrine of the Person of Christ. In one place this
was said to be "Now in the Publisher's hands."[2] The volume,
however, for some reason, never did see the light of day.

At about the time of the outbreak of the issues in Biblical
Criticism raised by William Robertson Smith, MacGregor
contributed an article in the April 1877 issue of *The British and
Foreign Evangelical Review* on "The Age of the Pentateuch, with
special reference to Revelation and Inspiration." This had
been first given as an address to a Free Church Clerical
Association in Edinburgh on 15th January 1877.[3] Whilst he
states that technically, or theologically, the Mosaic authorship
of the Pentateuch was not a Church dogma, MacGregor
nevertheless in his article makes a strong case for just that: the
Mosaic authorship of the Pentateuch. He makes his own
position clear at the outset: "My present opinion is, that in the
only sense felt important by intelligent advocates of the view

---

[2] On the fly-leaf of his 1890 pamphlet, *Presbyterians on Trial by their Principles.*
This was also referred to in an obituary notice in the *Christian Outlook* on
20th October 1894.
[3] James MacGregor, *Studies in the History of Christian Apologetics,* Edinburgh,
1894, 339.

that Moses wrote the Pentateuch, the writer of the Pentateuch was Moses; and that this will come to be the settled conviction of the people of God when they have gone through the process of real ascertainment."[4]

There are some *prima facie* reasons for the presumption of Mosaic authorship, according to MacGregor. On the one hand there is clear testimony in the Bible itself which presupposes this, and none which suggest a post-Mosaic authorship. There is also the presumption arising from the traditional widespread belief of the Church. Denials of Mosaic authorship only derived from the past 200 years of so. MacGregor refutes arguments arising from supposed sources, whether or not Moses could write, and the Hebrew style of the books. But he is particularly concerned to state the positive reasons for accepting Mosaic authorship:

(1) The first five books are just such as you would expect from the hand of Moses. Their structure indicates just such a context. MacGregor explains: "They look back to Egypt as of 'yesterday,' and look round on the Sinaitic peninsula as of 'to-day'; and, to the last, look forward to Canaan as of 'tomorrow.' "[5]

(2) "The *literature and history of Israel after Moses* appear to be at least consistent with, if not demand, the supposition that the Pentateuchal scriptures and institutions are Mosaic in their origin."[6] This is evident, believes MacGregor, in the

---

[4] James MacGregor, "Age of the Pentateuch, with Special Reference to Revelation and Inspiration," *The British and Foreign Evangelical Review*, Vol. XXVI, No. C, April 1877, 257. That this remained his firm opinion is clear from his later volume on *Exodus, Part I*, Edinburgh, 1889, 57-63.
[5] ibid., 267.
[6] ibid., 268.

subsequent references in the Old Testament canon to the "Law," the "Book of the Law," and the "Law of Moses," terms invariably referring to the Pentateuch.

(3) Then there is *the testimony of Christ Himself*. "There is hardly a noteworthy incident recorded in the five books down to the death of Moses that is not referred to by our Lord in such a way as to attest its reality."[7]

MacGregor did believe that enquiry into such an issue as Pentateuchal authorship was to be encouraged. He did feel, however, that this would only serve to bring out the fallacies of the critical positions. For example, writes MacGregor, to those who accept the inspiration of Scripture as God's Word, "it will appear in the last degree unlikely that God in Christ should have so spoken as *in effect* to mislead men about the human authorship of the Pentateuch."[8] Furthermore, they "will regard as incredible the suggestion that God should have moved any one but Moses to write a book so ostensibly Mosaic as Deuteronomy. The supposition that the Pentateuchal institutions are in large measure post-Mosaic will in like manner appear quite incredible."[9] MacGregor deals severely with the notion that Deuteronomy was to be considered as the production of a personator of Moses. The idea that he was not the author of Deuteronomy would not deceive the people of God in subsequent ages. The people would know the quasi-Moses was not the real Moses. They would not likely receive the production of a personator of Moses. "What is more likely is," says MacGregor, "that they

---

[7] ibid., 269.
[8] ibid., 271.
[9] ibid.

would stone the personator as profane."[10] After all, "it is inconceivable that *God* should have inspired or authorised any man to put on *the false face* of the supposed impersonation, if not for the purpose, to the effect, of leading many following generations to believe what is not true – that Moses said and did what he really did not say or do."[11]

MacGregor perceptively goes on to speak about the impact of evolutionism in influencing Biblical interpretation. The problem in this case is the influence of the "anti-supernaturalistic and infidel." There is an obvious distaste for the supernatural in such evolutionism, so that "supernatural communication to man, except in a measure infinitesimally small, would involve a violence to the nature of man's mind as rational."[12] This MacGregor cannot accept. He firmly believed that the permission and encouragement by the Church of friendly discussion would lead brethren "to recognise theoretically what they know in their own heart's experience, that the Bible does not record a series of illusive representations of ideas; that what it records is a historical proceeding of the living God towards the redemption of mankind."[13] He did not calculate, however, on the willingness of such 'brethren' to accept the "anti-supernaturalistic and infidel" approach, which would consequently leave a sad legacy of a denial of the inspiration and authority of the Bible.

Another issue which James MacGregor addressed was that of creedal subscription. Again, it was in the columns of *The*

---

[10] ibid.
[11] ibid., 271-2.
[12] ibid., 273.
[13] ibid., 274.

British and Foreign Evangelical Review that he made his
contribution in this area. The issue was in the air mainly on
account of the moves being made in the United Presbyterian
Church to adopt a Declaratory Act by which the terms of
Confessional subscription might effectively be modified in
specific areas of Confessional teaching. No doubt there were
also those in the Free Church who felt such 'relief' was
necessary from supposedly harsher aspects of Confessional
teaching. Change was in the air. MacGregor begins his
discussion on creedal subscription by asserting the legitimacy
of a Church revising or replacing its creed. It is obviously
important that there be honesty in such a thing and that a
Church should not retain a creed or confession it does not
believe. Instead of being a *bonâ fide* confession of its faith it
could become a *"malâ fide* concealment of incoherency or
dubitation." MacGregor's position is that "It is to the good
cause a great calamity if a church lapse from the belief of
Christian truths once ascertained and professed. But a
continued profession of adherence to articles of faith no
longer believed would be, not an alleviation, but an
aggravation, of the calamity."[14] He is aware that tensions may
exist within Churches on account of different types of
theological thinking within the Church. With reference to the
Free Church he makes the remarkable statement that, "There
are two types of theological thinking in our church – liberal
and conservative – as there always must be in any church of

---

[14]James MacGregor, "On Revision of the Westminster Confession," *The
British and Foreign Evangelical Review*, Vol. XXVI, No. CII, October 1877,
693.

living men."[15] Presumably he means by this a sort of spectrum within the fairly narrow confines of the Confessional Church. Unfortunately, in the Free Church the liberal element prevailed and the denomination experienced a marked theological downgrade by the end of the century. In terms of the Confessional position MacGregor was aware, however, that there was diversity in the Church, from those who would have absolutely no change at any price, and those who would be happy with significant qualifications of the standards.

Some seemed to believe that the *Westminster Confession* was too elaborate and that there would be an enlargement of freedom expected in changes in the form of confessional statements. The sort of change envisaged, by most who desired change, would not be in the direction of enlargement, but the opposite – shortening and simplifying. But MacGregor points out that such shortening would not necessarily involve enlarged freedoms. He shows that the reverse might be the case, for where there is something abbreviated and indefinite in form there could well be all sorts of arguments about the precise meaning of words, or doctrines believed and standards to be maintained. "The fact that a short and simple creed," says MacGregor, "so short and simple as to be confessedly elliptical, tends towards despotism, has not, I think, been sufficiently recognised in recent discussions, although individuals have found that their ministerial freedom is most effectively shielded by an elaborate confession – a confession so elaborate that the church does not feel bound, nor free, to go beyond its express articulations for purposes of discipline. I

---

[15] ibid., 694.

therefore give to the fact the emphasis of iteration."[16] However, the restraint on ministerial freedom itself is not constituted by the *form* of the confession, but the *substance* of the faith it confesses. "To be a Christian church – this faith of hers must always operate as a restraint upon freedom, both of communion and of ministration."[17] What limits may be suggested for just how elaborate a confession might be in a church? Proper criteria are required. MacGregor suggests two things:

(1) In terms of *Administration* a church must have a common understanding about certain things affecting its life. There will be things which must go into a confession though they may not be of the substance of Christian faith. MacGregor uses the example of the practice of infant baptism in a paedobaptist church. Confessing this does not require us to believe that the anti-paedobaptists are non-Christian. It is simply saying, this is our understanding of the teaching of Scripture and therefore an anti-paedobaptist cannot be a minister or office-bearer in our church. The work and administration of a church cannot go on without such positions being clear. Then,

(2) in terms of *Attainments* there is the point that taking the wider view there is the profession of those things which over time and history God's church has come to "attain" by way of doctrine and practice and government. MacGregor mentions as examples the doctrine of justification by faith as an "attainment" of Protestant Christendom. In addition, there are the doctrines of man's inability and sovereign grace, and even the question of the church's spiritual independence. A

---

[16] ibid., 700.
[17] ibid., 700-1.

church, in other words, will have an eye to what has been *attained* in doctrinal understanding from the past.

These two things together, maintains MacGregor, "will suffice as a regulative test of the legitimacy of detailed articulations in a church's confession of her faith."[18] On the basis of this (he says) "I think that we ought to retain the Westminster Confession as the confession of our common faith. I so think because I regard it as a superlatively good statement of what is commonly believed among us, and because it would be extremely difficult, perhaps practically impossible, to get another confession half so good that would be the received symbol, the visible connecting bond of that great Presbyterian empire on which the sun never sets, now visibly and sensibly connected by means of the venerable symbol of Westminster."[19] It is the case that retention of the *Confession* tends greatly towards deep, and wide, and strong theological thinking on the part of the churches holding to it. Would any proposed replacement be as good, or be so respected? That is not at all likely. To throw away such a confessional statement is, therefore, to throw away a very real advantage.

MacGregor goes on to consider some specific areas where objections were commonly raised:

(1) In relation to the *six days of creation*, he points out that the reference in the *Confession* is simply a Bible statement. He tends, however, in this article,[20] and his later article on "The

---

[18] ibid., 702.
[19] ibid., 703.
[20] ibid., 706.

Christian Doctrine of Creation,"[21] to be happy with an 'accommodation' to long ages or epochs as represented by the 'days.' In relation to "the theory that the 'days' of creation are epochs, of great and indefinite extent," he states in one article that "the present writer may be allowed to mention that this theory was embraced by him before he had given any serious attention to the relative ascertainments of geologic science."[22] This was, however, a common approach then in the face of the "assured results of modern science," which, they believed, required great quantities of time applied to the commonly received 'geological column.' In the early Free Church, even before the Darwinian era, such influential men as Thomas Chalmers and Hugh Miller advanced the idea of the necessity of great ages in earth's history. In many ways this was a crux, and the tendency to accommodate to secular science in this area tended to undermine in the public eye the credibility of the plain Biblical account of creation *ex nihilo*. It is true that MacGregor in one place says that "Christians…while giving interested attention to the processes and results of science, ought not to be quick to take alarm on account of these. 'He that believeth shall not make haste.'"[23] Though he was cautious in being dogmatic on the question of the understanding of Genesis 1, and certainly wished to stress the supernaturalism of the work of Creation, MacGregor was inclined to accept a "continuous creation" theory in which

---

[21] James MacGregor, "The Christian Doctrine of Creation," *The British and Foreign Evangelical Review*, Vol. XXVII, No. CVI, October 1878, 724-751.

[22] "The Christian Doctrine of Creation. III." *The Christian Treasury*, Edinburgh, 1872, 399.

[23] James MacGregor, "The Christian Doctrine of Creation," *The British and Foreign Evangelical Review*, Vol. XXVII, No. CVI, October 1878, 750.

creation is represented as "proceeding through an ascending series of stages, and terminating in the Creator's rest."[24] All the theorising on how to understand Genesis 1 in the light of science, however, tended to give little weight to the plain meaning of the text of Genesis. After all, why was so much time necessary? Would there not be an 'appearance of age'? Once the 'geological column' was accepted, within the framework of uniformitarian science and consequent long ages of death and decay before man came on the scene, how could it be said in relation, for example, to the work of the "six days" that "it was very good" (Genesis 1:31)?[25] And how could any concession to evolutionary development be squared with the distinctness of man as a being specially formed in the image of God (Genesis 1:26-28)?

(2) In relation to the questions raised about whether *infant damnation* was taught in the *Confession* with reference to "elect infants dying in infancy"[26] MacGregor argues that the *Confession* simply teaches that in such a case, – as well as in the case of "other elect persons, who are incapable of being called by the outward ministry of the word,"[27] that is to say those among the heathen and mentally ill – any who may be saved will be saved by sovereign grace according to the electing purpose of God. The *Confession* speaks prudently, without

---

[24] ibid., 747. See also page 748, and page 750 where he says that this view "is most likely to prove the correct one."

[25] For an excellent modern conservative approach to the straightforward understanding of the days in Genesis 1, see Douglas F. Kelly's *Creation and Change. Genesis 1:1 – 2:4 in the light of changing scientific paradigms*, Fearn, 1997. See also Jonathan Sarfati's refutation of "Progressive Creationism," *Refuting Compromise*, Green Forest, AR, 2004.

[26] *Confession of Faith*, X:III.

[27] ibid.

stating either that all infants dying in infancy are necessarily lost or that none are.[28] Similarly in the case of "others." However, as MacGregor points out, with reference to the way salvation is wrought in every case: "the theological interest of the divines here lies in asserting that the only source of salvation is God's grace, and that the only legal ground of it is His righteousness in Christ. Hence, they oppose the suggestion that 'virtuous' heathens can be saved by their virtues, that they have been elected on account of those virtues foreseen, or justified on the ground of those virtues realised."[29]

(3) In relation to *reprobation* objections were made that the *Confession* taught this and that it was harsh and incompatible with God's love. The word of course did not appear in the *Confession*, but the truth was there, namely, that the non-elect have been "ordained…to dishonour and wrath for their sin."[30] MacGregor argues against denials or scruples about reprobation on three grounds: (a) Apart from an unacceptable universalism, it is a fact; there is an abandonment of some to wrath and dishonour on account of sin. (b) What God does in time, He must have planned to do from eternity. (c) Once an election is recognised, it must be admitted that the non-elect must be doomed on account of their sin. "No real Calvinist can have any difficulty," MacGregor maintains, "in accepting

---

[28] James MacGregor, "On the Revision of the Westminster Confession," 706-7.
[29] ibid., 708. Cf. *Confession of Faith*, X:IV.
[30] *Confession of Faith*, III:VII.

the confessional statement regarding the destiny of the non-elect as doomed to death eternal for their sins."[31]

Supposing the *Confession* should be retained, the question arises as to the manner in which it is to be retained. James MacGregor would wish it to be retained "pure and simple." At the same time he says that he has a measure of sympathy with the rescission of some parts, such as what the Americans did in relation to the Civil Magistrate. He is not altogether averse to the suggestion for declaratory Acts, but only "in so far as these declaratory acts mean, not interpretation, but effective supersession."[32] He does not like the suggestion that there should be a lesser creed for elders and deacons. On the one hand it suggests the unfortunate presumption of a want of mental or spiritual ability to grasp the *Confession* of their part, something such office bearers might resent, especially as seemingly placing them on a lower ecclesiastical level. That would not be healthy for a church. MacGregor does not like, either, any idea of relaxing the form of subscription. Rather than subscribing the "whole doctrine" of the *Confession* some apparently thought it would be easier to simply subscribe the "substance" or "system" of the *Confession*.[33] But why should an honest man scruple about the whole doctrine if he can hold the substance or system? MacGregor, however, is suspicious that "those vague expressions ["system" or "substance"] are liable to most formidable abuse."[34] His conclusion is that what

---

[31] James MacGregor, "On the Revision of the Westminster Confession," 708.
[32] ibid., 709.
[33] ibid., 711.
[34] ibid.

is intended by the prescribed form of adherence should be
provided for "by a form which admits no misapprehension."[35]

MacGregor also counters the suggestion that there should
be a short and simple creed in place of the more detailed one.
Such documents could not, however, effectively serve the
purposes of a Church's Confession. For how could they really
show what all the ministers are bound to teach on behalf of
the Church, when the statements would be so attenuated and
inexplicit? No, there is a great advantage in having a
Confession as detailed as the *Westminster Confession of Faith*, and
retaining it more or less just as it is. Whatever the
disadvantages may be, "those greater advantages, secured in
part by having a non-scriptural form of sound words, are
secured most completely by having a form as nearly as
possible unchanging."[36]

James MacGregor wrote prolifically in this period. His
contributions were nothing if they were not thought
provoking. There was originality about much of his work. At
the same time there is little "interacting with contemporary
scholarship" evident on the face of his written work. No
doubt such interaction is necessary. But it may also have the
effect of quickly dating works. MacGregor no doubt made
himself familiar with contemporary scholarship – the extent of
his reading is evident especially in his last volume on *Studies in
the History of Christian Apologetics*. However, he tended to *write*
simply according to his considered convictions on whatever
issue he tackled. In addition, there is no mistaking his
conservative bent. He frequently wrote for *The British and*

---

[35] ibid.
[36] ibid., 713.

Foreign Evangelical Review, probably the premier Review in Britain at that time on the evangelical side. Between 1868 and his departure for New Zealand in 1881 he contributed no less than eleven major articles amounting to some 270 pages. His distinctly conservative and Calvinistic perspective is clear from his articles on "The Catholic Doctrine of the Atonement" (February 1871), "Dr. William Cunningham" (October 1871), and "Dr. Charles Hodge and the Princeton School" (July 1874). In fact, these were extended book reviews respectively of Dr Hugh Martin's work on the *Atonement*, the *Biography* of Dr Cunningham by James Mackenzie and Robert Rainy, and the monumental three-volume *Systematic Theology* by Charles Hodge, which was completed in 1873. MacGregor was obviously very much in the same school theologically as Cunningham and Hodge, whose books he used in his own classes. Besides this there is his "Nature of the Divine Inspiration of Scripture" (April 1880) in which he deals among other things with difficulties of apparent inaccuracies in Scripture. MacGregor deals with these in a competent and orthodox way. He would take them up later in his volume *The Revelation and the Record*, which finally appeared in 1893.

His writings contained some erratic aspects, but on the whole showed him to be a competent conservative theologian with a concern for the issues that were thrusting themselves upon the Church in that era. His writings, on the whole, still make profitable reading. It is a pity that his projected book on the *Person of Christ* never saw the light of day and is now "lost," for it may well have been the book of popular and abiding appeal which is missing from his later published work.

For the greater part in their time in Edinburgh the MacGregors resided at 'Harmony House,' Eden Lane, in the Morningside area of the city. The sadness noted by Norman Macfarlane no doubt refers to the deaths by tuberculosis in Edinburgh of MacGregor's two oldest children, Georgina (at 16 in 1874) and Duncan (at 18 in 1878). Another son, James, showed signs of that affliction. Such problems with his own health and that of his family constrained him to tender his resignation from the Chair in a letter of 29th March 1881 to the College Committee. He says in that letter: "Domestic circumstances, especially those affecting the health of my children and myself, incline me to offer to resign my chair for the purposes of seeking work in a more congenial climate. New Zealand is what is thought of."[37] Submitted with the letter was a letter from his medical advisor, Andrew Smart of 14 Charlotte Square, stating his opinion that in the interests of the health of himself and certain of his family he should seek "a complete and permanent change of climate." "I am most hopeful," he says, "that, under God's blessing, such a change would be the means of warding off the danger, which in this country threatens your family." Smart was under the unhesitating opinion that New Zealand should be his destination. The College Committee at its meeting of 6th April 1881 resolved to accept the resignation, and with the end of the Session that year came the end of James MacGregor's Professorial labours in the New College, completing thirteen years' service.

[37] *PDGAFCS*, May 1881, Report of College Committee. May 1881. No. V. 2.

After his resignation James MacGregor received many words of appreciation from his contemporaries. Among letters received was this one from the Rev. Alexander Whyte, minister of the prestigious Free St. George's congregation in Edinburgh's west end and a leading churchman of the day and fellow-Presbyter with MacGregor in Edinburgh:

52, Melville Street, Edinburgh,   June 6th, 1881.

My Dear Dr MacGregor,—Although I in common with all your friends must acquiesce in your decision to leave Edinburgh and take your family to a more genial climate, yet it is not without much pain that we consent to part with you. For myself your departure is the loss of a familiar friendship that has been from its beginning most pleasant and most valuable to me. Your wide reading, your philosophical habit of mind, your profound grasp of Scriptural truth, and your vivid, original, and entirely individual way of stating your views and beliefs,– all these things have often told with great effect on my mind. And the singular nobility, generosity, and chivalry of your character, has many a time rebuked the much lower temper of mind it found in me. Altogether, your friendship has been full of good fruits for myself.

As to your preaching, it is no exaggeration to say that it is quite unique in the display of those qualities which make your conversation and correspondence so valuable. The hold you have of the doctrines of grace, and the fresh, flashing, vividly *experimental* way you have of setting them forth in pulpit expositions,–these remarkable qualities have always made your preaching most interesting and most helpful to the best of my people. Altogether your removal from the Edinburgh pulpit, and from our social and religious circle, will be a deep and long-felt loss to many. You must pardon me for writing as I have done, but I could not let you

leave us without some such expression of my gratitude
and affection.
Believe me, always, dear Dr MacGregor,
Most truly yours,
(Signed) Alexander Whyte

These touching words are a fitting reflection on MacGregor's whole ministry and his professorial work in Scotland, highlighting as they do some of the distinct qualities and gifts employed in his Master's service. However, for himself and his family a new chapter was opening up which would take them to the opposite side of the world.

10

SOUTHWARD BOUND

On the advice of his Doctor, and for the protection of the health of himself and his family, James MacGregor set sail with his family on the *Jessie Readman* from Greenock on 15th July 1881, and disembarked at Port Chalmers, just north of Dunedin in the South Island of New Zealand, on 24th October that same year, after a journey of 100 days. The *Jessie Readman* was an iron ship of some 962 tons, a sailing ship with three masts and rigging. It had been built by Scott of Greenock for Patrick Henderson & Co. in 1869 with the purpose of being a settler or migrant ship on the route from Scotland to New Zealand.[1] The Captain on that passage out was a Mr Gibson. There were 101 passengers on the journey. The MacGregors were among 15 who travelled Saloon class. James and Grace MacGregor's two oldest children, Georgina (at 16) and Duncan (at 18), had died in Edinburgh of *tuberculosis*. But with them on the way to New Zealand were their two surviving sons, William Cunningham and James, and six daughters, Helen, Agnes, Grace, Catherine, Margaret and

---

[1] James MacGregor, *The Revelation and the Record*, Edinburgh, 1893, 194. On the journey out to New Zealand MacGregor's second oldest surviving daughter, Agnes Susan Craig MacGregor (born 24th June, 1867), kept a Diary of experiences on the ship (and afterwards, family life in Dunedin and Oamaru). Copies of this Diary are found in various places in New Zealand, most notably in the National Library.

Charlotte. Of his children, three of the daughters – Agnes (1962), Grace (1963) and Charlotte (1966) – lived to a good old age. Sadly, James, born in Paisley in 1863, died of *tuberculosis* on the passage out.

The *Jessie Readman* was the sister ship of the Christian McCauseland. Built by Scott of Greenock for Patrick Henderson's Albion Line, she was a vessel of 962 tons. The MacGregor family sailed to New Zealand on this vessel in 1881.

On arriving in New Zealand, the MacGregor family lived for the first five months in Dunedin. James MacGregor automatically became a minister without a charge in the Synod of Otago and Southland. The South Island was largely a Scottish colony, and largely a Free Church settlement. After the Disruption of 1843 plans were set in foot to plant a Free Church colony in Otago. With a view to becoming minister to the emigrants, the Rev. Thomas Burns resigned his charge in Monkton, Ayrshire. However, war in the colony delayed the immigration and in 1846 Burns took the charge of Portobello

Free Church near Edinburgh. He was not long there, though, as the following year he did set off with other Free Church emigrants to plant the proposed colony in Otago. Burns (1796-1871) was a nephew of the famous Scottish poet, Robert Burns. He was the only minister in the Otago colony up to 1854. "The ecclesiastical leader of the Free Church Settlement of Otago, Dr Burns for nearly a quarter of a century exercised a commanding influence over the Colony, in the founding of which he played so conspicuous a part."[2]

For a few months after arriving in Otago James MacGregor supplied congregations in the then sparsely-settled outback of Southland, between Invercargill and Kingston, on the southern shores of Lake Wakatipu. Shortly after his arrival he was asked how he liked the colony. He replied: "Immensely. All that I see strikes me at once with wonder and delight. I am especially struck, so that I can hardly believe my eyes, by the maturity and completeness of things here, in town and country. But I am more deeply impressed by the conditions affecting the permanent prosperity of a community. Yours is truly a 'good land,' in the sense in which that description was applied to Palestine of old...A Scotchman of the old school sees with delight, here realised for the first time in history, John Knox's idea of national education..."[3]

---

[2] William Ewing (Editor), *Annals of the Free Church of Scotland, 1843-1900*, Volume 1, Edinburgh, 1914, 110.

[3] James MacGregor, *Balquhidder, Rob Roy, &c.*, Dunedin, [1882], 1.

Columba Church, Oamaru, where James MacGregor ministered from 1882 until his passing in 1894.

Not long after arriving MacGregor was called to take charge of a new congregation in Oamaru. This was the second charge in the town and was a result of a growth in the population of the place. At first a preaching station was established in 1879, but in 1882 this developed into a congregation and on 23rd March that year James MacGregor was inducted to the charge. It is said that the occasion of his induction created considerable public interest that 348 persons were happy to pay 2/- each for admission to a welcome 'Soiree' in the evening.[4] The congregation was originally called 'Oamaru South.' However, the name 'Columba Church' was used by the Rev. D. M. Stuart (Dunedin) at the welcome meeting for James MacGregor. Apparently, the minutes of a meeting of managers of 17th April [1882] recorded that "It is

---

[4] *Columba Presbyterian Church. Centennial 1881-1981*, 6.

agreed that the name of the Church be COLUMBA CHURCH."[5]. The first charge in the town was called St Paul's, but the story goes that MacGregor was averse to the use of "St" for his own congregation and it was consequently the modest "Columba Church"!

A Church building made of Oamaru stone located at the corner of Wansbeck and Ure Streets, built by one Duncan Sutherland in classical style to the design of Forrester and Lemon, was opened on 15th July 1883.[6] The building was in a plain, rectangular Basilica style and was capable of seating 800 people. The north-facing façade was impressive, comprising four Doric columns flanked by two square Doric pillars.[7] The final cost amounted to some £4,500.[8] This was a huge sum for those days and was met predominantly by the congregation, though the Synod of Otago and Southland contributed £1,500.[9] It was said that the St Paul's and Columba Presbyterian Churches were ornaments to the town.

Oamaru was the third town in size in Otago after Dunedin. It had about 6,000 inhabitants in those days and was 75 miles north of Dunedin. The town was built of white stone quarried locally. Inevitably it became known by the name

---

[5] ibid., 8.

[6] Ian Breward, 'MacGregor, James,' from *the Dictionary of New Zealand Biography*, Te Ara – the Encyclopedia of New Zealand, updated 12-Nov-2013 (http://www.TeAra.govt.nz/en/biographies/2m8/macgregor-james, accessed 27 March 2014). See also C. Stuart Ross, *The Story of the Otago Church and Settlement*, Dunedin, 1887, 375-376; J. Collie, *The Story of the Otago Free Church Settlement*, Dunedin, 1948, 111; and *Columba Presbyterian Church. Centennial 1881-1981*, 8.

[7] Gavin McLean, *Oamaru. History & Heritage*, Dunedin 2002, 49.

[8] *Columba Presbyterian Church. Centennial 1881-1981*, 8.

[9] ibid.

"White City." It appears that the town flourished in a gold
prospecting boom in the middle years of the nineteenth
century. Positioned on the south-east coast of the South
Island, Oamaru had a breakwater one thousand eight hundred
and fifty feet long, with an enclosure of sixty acres. It was
extended to accommodate ocean-going ships, but
unfortunately, it is said, the extension bankrupted the town!
This hit the Presbyterian congregations. Columba Church was
made to seat 800, but initially only 189 sittings were let.
Oamaru did not grow as anticipated and economic depression
hit the town. In 1885, embarrassingly, a salary cheque of £75
paid to James MacGregor was dishonoured by the Bank. The
following year once again the managers recorded that there
were insufficient funds to pay the minister's salary, though a
John McLean of Redcastle donated an amount of £50 to
'balance the books.'[10] It is also recorded that in 1888
MacGregor's stipend was reduced from £300 to £220![11]
Perhaps this explains MacGregor's submission of an Essay on
"Socialism and its bearings on Capital, Labour, and Poverty"
for the Fraser Theological Prize (Sydney) in November 1889.
In the event he shared the prize of £100 with a Rev. Mr
Houston of Whangarei.[12] The Essay of MacGregor's was
published in three different Theological Journals.[13]

---

[10] *Columba Presbyterian Church. Centennial 1881-1981*, 41.
[11] ibid. Ian Breward, 'MacGregor, James,' from *the Dictionary of New Zealand Biography*, Te Ara – the Encyclopedia of New Zealand, updated 12-Nov-2013 (http://www.TeAra.govt.nz/en/biographies/2m8/macgregor-james, accessed 27 March 2014).
[12] *Columba Presbyterian Church. Centennial 1881-1981*, 40.
[13] See items 64, 65, and 66 in the *Bibliography (A)* of James MacGregor's Published Writings, on page 203 below.

Oamaru had several large flour mills and a freezing establishment capable of freezing eight hundred sheep a day and storage for twenty thousand carcasses. "A very long and wide street passes through the centre of the town with some excellent stores," said the Rev. Donald MacDougall in 1899.[14] MacDougall adds other contemporary details of Oamaru and its environs: "The country for many miles around it is rich and beautiful. It produces the best wheat, oats and potatoes in New Zealand. The average yield of wheat in 1898 was thirty-two bushels per acre, of oats thirty seven, barley thirty three, and rye twenty seven…From twenty to fifty miles back into the mountains is a great grazing country, well adapted for sheep and cattle. Some of the runs in the hill country are capable of carrying twenty thousand sheep."[15] Apparently the district of Otago was a great exporter of rabbit skins, being responsible for providing 30% of the 15,229,314 skins exported from New Zealand in 1898! It was a farming area, with a rabbit problem but a pleasant climate, and it was after all a Presbyterian country. Rabbits, however, were not the only problem. Of the lifestyle of the rabbiters MacGregor was scathing: "They not only never go to church, but work on at their trade on Sabbath…some are married, and, as they can make plenty of money, their wives and children can live in style."[16]

---

[14] Donald MacDougall, *The Conversion of the Maoris*, Philadelphia, 1899, 214. Much of the detail in this chapter about Oamaru at that time has been taken from the account given by MacDougall in this book, page 213 and following.

[15] ibid., 214.

[16] Jennie Coleman, "Beyond Theology", *Touchstone*, May 2002 (from www.archives.presbyterian.org.nz / page230.htm).

One almost amusing incident arising from his ministry at Oamaru was a question of the legitimacy of the weddings he conducted. It appears that he had been conducting marriages whilst he was not on the list of officiating ministers. This necessitated an Act to be entered into Parliament in 1889 just for himself in order to remove doubts as to the validity of every marriage conducted by him up to that point![17]

For the amusement of his family James MacGregor was wont to write 'nonsense verse,' not least on some of the curiosities of New Zealand natural history. Of the moa he wrote:

> The moa's extinct,
> He didn't live long in this New Zealand clime,
> The reason for that is because, I think,
> He lived too long at a time –
> That is, ten feet!

The kiwi also had its turn:

> The little Kiwi,
> He pleases me.
> He hasn't got any wings, I suppose,
> So he wants to make the most of his nose.
> So when he, himself, would fain dispose
> For a night of sweet and deep repose,
> In the ground, as you know, he sticks his nose
> And then no more than this word he throws
> Over his shoulder, "Goodnight mama, here goes!"[18]

---

[17] For details of this Act see: http://legislation.knowledge-basket.co.nz/shattering_statutes/1889/Otago_Marriages_1889.pdf (accessed 12th January, 2015).

[18] These verses were provided by Mrs A.D. Kerr (née Patterson), a granddaughter of James MacGregor, in a letter to the author dated 19th April 1972. Agnes Kerr was a daughter of Catherine, third youngest of James and Grace MacGregor's daughters.

This provides a flavour of the situation James MacGregor experienced as he and his remaining family settled in their adopted country.

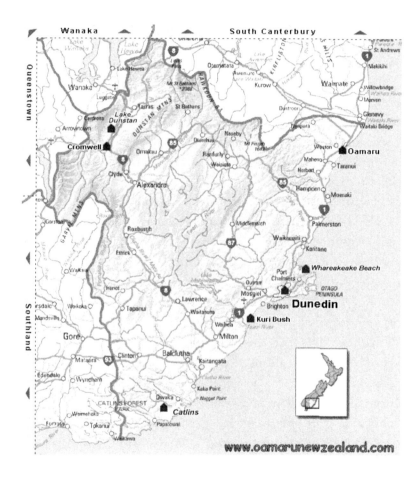

11

THE WAITAKI SCHOOL CONTROVERSY

James MacGregor made a lasting impression throughout Otago because of his remarkable gifts. "He had a rugged strength of personality and could be a formidable controversialist."[1] It goes without saying that his interests centred on his ministry at Columba Church in Oamaru, and the wider concerns of the life of the Church in Otago and Southland. In relation to wider social issues he became involved in the provision of education in the district. This involved him in some controversy. No doubt it became such a serious issue because a high school education for his six daughters was, as he saw it, clearly threatened.

The heart of the controversy involved the Waitaki High School, an institution which had been established by Act of Parliament and had been endowed with public land. The school was built about a mile and a half outside the then Oamaru boundary. The early governors, who included two Etonians, envisaged as close a model of an English public school as was possible under colonial conditions. A well-qualified Rector was imported from England, and a scale of fees was fixed which, while not unreasonable, was beyond the

---

[1] Ian Breward, 'MacGregor, James,' from *the Dictionary of New Zealand Biography*, Te Ara — the Encyclopedia of New Zealand, updated 12-Nov-2013 (http://www.TeAra.govt.nz/en/biographies/2m8/macgregor-james, accessed 27 March 2014).

reach of the average New Zealand parent. The school, which from the first admitted boarders, was opened in 1883.

The new school aroused a good deal of hostility in Oamaru, where secondary education was already available at what was known as the Oamaru District High School. This was merely a primary school with attached secondary classes. For the latter fees were charged, but only a fifth of those demanded at Waitaki. The ill-feeling towards Waitaki was due (a) to the belief that it was a class school wrongfully endowed from public resources, (b) to its classical curriculum, (c) to its lack of provision for girls, and (d) to its distance from the town. The matter became acute when the Otago Education Board, which controlled the national system in the province, proposed in 1883 to abolish the upper classes at the District High School on the grounds that it was now the responsibility of the Waitaki Governors to provide for secondary education in North Otago. Since the Waitaki High School was a boys'-only establishment, this had the effect of depriving a large number of children, including all girls, of access to higher education.

James MacGregor hurled himself into the fray with enthusiasm as he took the lead in the defence of the District High School, making representations to the Education Board and obtaining a reprieve for it for a year. In the meantime, he was elected through the local School Committee to a seat on the Otago Education Board. After the year of grace the District High School was disrated for a time, but MacGregor was able to persuade the Board to carry it on as a District High School for two more years "or until endowments for the Waitaki High School are applied to their proper purpose."

Throughout the controversy he not only wrote his customary lengthy letters to the press, but, more practically, he organised an impressive movement to have Waitaki disestablished and its endowments used for the support of the District High School. In this he almost succeeded. "In November, 1885, he convened a Conference of representatives of school committees throughout North Otago, and before it he laid a plan for the removal of the school [Waitaki] to the town, the foundation of a commercial site, the reduction of fees to £2 a year, and the grant of free education to deserving pupils. The conference agreed to the proposals and set up a committee to try to put them into effect."[2] As a first measure a vote of householders throughout the district was taken, and was declared to result in favour of the resolution by 709 to 61! By means of such conferences, approaches to public bodies, and opinion polls, James MacGregor gained a very large measure of support.

Having got himself elected to the Otago Education Board he was then appointed its representative on the Waitaki Board. At this stage he had good hopes of carrying his proposals on the Waitaki Board itself, and was only foiled by an unexpected *volte face* on the part of one of the Governors. He presented a petition to Parliament which eventually appointed a Commission of inquiry into the whole situation. J. Shepherd and W. Montgomery were the commissioners appointed by Parliament and they conducted their

---

[2] K. C. McDonald, *History of Otago*, Oamaru: Published under the auspices of the North Otago Centennial Committee, 1940, 159. Much of the information provided here on this issue derives from Mr McDonald's work.

investigation in Oamaru in January 1887, when many witnesses were examined. Meanwhile MacGregor had been occupied in placing before the public descriptions of two Scottish schools which he regarded as models – Dollar Academy and Madras College, St Andrews. The Report of the Commission was issued in March 1887. It recommended that, in view of the expenditure already incurred on the Waitaki High School, the suitability of the building, and the apparent healthiness of the site, the School should not be removed to the town. At the same time the Otago Education Board was urged to give attention to the "desirability of providing facilities for the higher education of girls."[3]

Throughout this controversy, which continued for some four years, one of MacGregor's chief opponents was Samuel Shrimski, the local Member of Parliament. Shrimski was a Polish Jew who had done well in business in Oamaru. He had been primarily responsible for having had the Waitaki High School Act passed. He had little knowledge of education, and his chief motive was probably to secure for North Otago endowments which might otherwise have gone to other districts. Having thus committed himself to the Waitaki project, however, he defended it with as much vigour as MacGregor displayed on the other side. Although he was not an invited delegate he attended one of the conferences convened by Dr MacGregor; but when he attempted to speak MacGregor, in the chair, accused him of interrupting the meeting and threatened to have him removed by the police. Afterwards a friend remarked to MacGregor that he had heard

---

[3] ibid., 160. On this issue see also K. C. McDonald, *White Stone Country – the Story of North Otago*, North Otago Centenary Committee, 1962, 203.

he had had an encounter with Shrimski. "Encounter? Encounter?" snorted the minister, "I just sne-e-ezed at the man!"

Although James MacGregor was greatly disappointed and surprised by the decision of the Commission in favour of the retention of Waitaki in its existing form and that the District High School was then disrated, at least he could claim that he had achieved something, for the Waitaki Board established a parallel school for girls and also founded a system of scholarships. In the long run, although MacGregor did not live to see it, Waitaki accepted the national scheme of free places for almost all its pupils, and developed into one of the most famous secondary schools in the country.

It may be said that the whole controversy was largely a clash between English and Scottish educational and social ideals, Dr MacGregor, himself a product of the Scottish system and a firm patriot, naturally took the side he was bred to, and with a good deal of justification.

With reference to Dr MacGregor the opinion of John Harkness, Waitaki's first Rector, who perhaps had little cause to praise him, should be recorded. Long afterwards, when Harkness was an old man, he wrote: "There was nothing paltry or nagging about him. He appeared to cherish no personal animosities, and didn't go about the country trying to do people injuries…he had no interest whatever in tale-bearing, gossip, or lobby intrigues. He did not revive controversies when they were over, or bear ill-will about attacks. I fancy he was really too big a man for Otago or even New Zealand."

It is of interest to note that somewhat later a 'North Otago Bible in Schools Association' was established at Oamaru on 8th June 1892. James MacGregor was appointed the first President of the Association. The purpose of the Association was clearly stated by the first two resolutions adopted at that first meeting:

> 1. "That in the National Education System of this country there ought to be permitted the reading of the Bible in the common schools, because it is desired by a majority of the people of the country on the ground that the Bible is God's word for mankind."
>
> 2. "That there ought to be permitted use of the Bible in schools, because the Bible is of singular value as an instrument of education and is a creative influence in the modern civilisation, such that to grow up in ignorance of it is to be not educated in that civilisation."[4]

MacGregor was concerned that the influence and use of the Bible in the Schools was not what it should be, and he lent his considerable weight to promoting the use of the Bible in Schools. The trouble was that in the Education Act of 1877 there was a secular clause.

Another person who took up this cause with enthusiasm was a protégé of James MacGregor's named Philadelphus Bain Fraser (1862-1940) who became the first Secretary of the Bible in Schools Association. Fraser, a Scotsman from Lerwick in Shetland, where his father, Daniel, had been Free

---

[4] Details of this first meeting are to be found in The Pamphlet Collection of Sir Robert Stout: Volume 70, on the web-site of Victoria University of Wellington: http://nzetc.victoria.ac.nz/tm/scholarly/tei-Stout70-t19-front-d2.html (accessed 12 January, 2016).

Church minister [1846-1872], was at first a teacher after he
arrived in New Zealand in 1885. He became editor of the *Bible
in Schools Advocate*. In 1892 he wrote an article which
effectively spells out his perspective: "Mental mutilation of the
people's children, by exclusion of the Bible from Schools."

That same year James MacGregor gave an address for the
Association in which he spoke of the disgrace of the exclusion
of the Bible from Schools. He called it "New Zealand's *Index
Expurgatorius*." He closed this published address with the
following remarks, the relevance of which have if anything
increased in the West in subsequent history:

> The secularism may to some extent be provided
> against otherwise. To a lamentably great extent it
> will not be provided against otherwise, than by
> having the Bible in the national schools. And what
> we as a nation have to do with is, the national
> provision, which at present is a provision, not for
> preventing a secularistic mindlessness in future
> citizens, but for secularising their education. Our
> plain straight open duty is, to set that matter right:
> making an end of the secularistic tyranny of a few
> political schemers; whose bad work has already
> brought on this nation the disgrace of persecuting
> religious belief through an *index expurgatorius*
> against the creative Book of the only real
> civilisation of the peoples, and has brought on the
> community the mischief that is folded in our
> having kept the Bible out of the education of half a
> generation of future citizens. Let those who are in
> earnest move in earnest, stirring up the languid,
> collecting the feeble sparks and fanning them into
> a flame. Let every elector say to the man who
> wants his vote, I will be influenced in my voting by
> your bearing toward this matter. Let all keep

storming at the door of Parliament until the
people's known mind become the nation's law.[5]

In 1892, under MacGregor's influence, Fraser became a
student for the ministry and subsequently a minister. Like his
mentor he opposed the union of the Synod of Otago and
Southland with the Presbyterian Church in New Zealand in
the north, which nevertheless came about in 1901, on a basis,
however, which allowed the Synod's continued autonomy.
Fraser was by all accounts a "doughty controversialist," and in
1909 he produced *A Brief Statement of the Reformed Faith*, a 24-
page booklet later re-issued in 1956 by the Westminster
Fellowship within the Presbyterian Church of New Zealand.[6]

---

[5]   ibid.:   http://nzetc.victoria.ac.nz/tm/scholarly/tei-Stout70-t19-body-
d1.html (accessed 12 January, 2016).
[6] For details of P. B. Fraser see, Allan K. Davidson. 'Fraser, Philadelphus
Bain,' from the *Dictionary of New Zealand Biography*, Te Ara – the
Encyclopedia of New Zealand, updated 25-Sep-2013:
http://www.TeAra.govt.nz/en/biographies/3f12/fraser-philadelphus-bain
(accessed 27 March 2014).

12

MR STANDFAST

In all James MacGregor had a thirteen-year ministry in Oamaru, in which, it was said, "he edified his own congregation by a style of preaching quite above the ordinary level."[1] The Centenary History of the congregation records that "The first minister had seen the Church grow and become established."[2] His influence, however, extended far beyond his own congregation. "He made a lasting impression throughout Otago because of his remarkable gifts."[3] This wider ministry was marked by two special features, not unrelated to one another, namely, his writings and his involvement in Church controversies arising on the one hand from a weakening of confessional doctrinal standards, and on the other hand by pressures for wider Church Union with the Presbyterian Church in New Zealand, which covered areas of New Zealand other than Otago and Southland.

James MacGregor and family had immigrated to the Antipodes immediately after the conclusion – if it may be said to be a conclusion – of the Robertson Smith Case. As we have

---

[1] R. G. Balfour, *Presbyterianism in the Colonies*, Edinburgh, 1899, 245.
[2] *Columba Presbyterian Church. Centennial 1881-1981*, 9.
[3] Ian Breward, 'MacGregor, James,' from *the Dictionary of New Zealand Biography*, Te Ara – the Encyclopedia of New Zealand, updated 12-Nov-2013 (http://www.TeAra.govt.nz/en/biographies/2m8/macgregor-james, accessed 27 March 2014).

indicated, the views propounded by Smith and other like-minded ministers and scholars had by then already taken root in the Churches, and not least in the theological halls. This cavalier approach to Scripture and its historicity and structure would have a serious impact on previously held views of Scripture authority. The Churches of course had to cope with the challenge of increasing secularisation and the rise of modern science, with its evolutionary dogmas. These trends seriously unsettled the Churches and were a contributing factor to the re-evaluation of Christian doctrine within the Churches. Under particular pressure were the doctrines of divine inspiration, creation, and, generally, the prophetic predictions and the miraculous. The rise of such views in science and literary criticism were not unrelated to one another, and were the occasion for a serious downgrade in the Churches.

We have seen how MacGregor addressed some of these issues in a fundamentally conservative way in a series of articles submitted to *The British and Foreign Evangelical Review* in the 1870s. Needless to say the sorts of church movements in Scotland were also felt in the Free Church influenced Synod of Otago and Southland into whose ministry MacGregor was admitted in 1881. By the time he travelled to New Zealand the United Presbyterian Church in Scotland had already – in 1879 – adopted a *Declaratory Act* intended to "relieve" sensitive scruples some ministers or elders may have entertained about Creation and Calvinism.

Three years after his settlement in Oamaru applications were invited from suitable candidates for the Chair of Mental and Moral Philosophy at the University of Otago. This arose from the forthcoming vacation of the Chair by one Duncan MacGregor, no relation to James. However it came about, James was encouraged to apply for this vacant position, in the course of which he gathered together various testimonials from Scotland and New Zealand in support of his case.[4] Among other applicants were two other Scots who were also ministers in the Synod of Otago and Southland, William Salmond (1835-1917) and James Copland (1834-1902), both, on the face of it, well-qualified men. Edinburgh-born Salmond was licensed in the United Presbyterian Church of Scotland before he became minister of a congregation of the English Presbyterian Church at North Shields, near Newcastle, around 1858. In 1876 he emigrated with his family from England to Dunedin in New Zealand to take up an appointment of professor in theology at the Presbyterian College there. By the time he moved to New Zealand he already had a reputation for holding fairly extreme heterodox opinions.[5]

By contrast to Salmond, James Copland and James MacGregor, other applicants for the Otago chair, were men of impeccable orthodoxy. Copland was something of a polymath. He studied arts and theology in Edinburgh and Berlin, obtained a PhD from Heidelberg University in 1858, and took the degree of MD at the University of Aberdeen in 1864. He

---

[4] These may be seen in *The Pamphlet Collection of Sir Robert Stout, Volume 65*, on the web-site of the Victoria University of Wellington Library: http://nzetc.victoria.ac.nz/tm/scholarly/tei-Stout65-t21.html   (accessed 27th March 2014).

[5] On William Salmond see Peter Matheson: 'Salmond, William,' from the *Dictionary of New Zealand Biography*, Te Ara – the Encyclopedia of New Zealand, updated 29-Jan-2014
(http://www.TeAra.govt.nz/en/biographies/2s3/salmond-william, accessed 27 March, 2014).

then became a licentiate of the United Presbyterian Church of Scotland. Copland immigrated to Otago in 1864-5 and took a charge in the goldfields town of Lawrence before in 1871 being called as the first Presbyterian minister in North Dunedin.[6] On a trip back to Scotland in 1874 he saw through the press a volume on the plenary inspiration of Scripture: *The Testimony Attested. A popular Manual of the evidence in support of the Authority and Inspiration of the Scriptures*.[7] The *Evangelical Presbyterian* commented of this book that "Dr Copland's position was that of the Westminster Confession: and his book received high praise from the Rev. C. H. Spurgeon, who thought it 'one of the most useful books we have seen for many a day...'"[8] Peter Matheson makes an interesting comment on a later work of Copland's: "His most important writing, *The origin and spiritual nature of man* (1885), penned as part of his unsuccessful candidacy for the chair of mental and moral philosophy at the University of Otago, argues cogently against Charles Darwin: concerned to defend the personal identity and moral nature of the self, he condemns evolution as both a materialist and reductionist reading of human life and an unrealistic, unproven hypothesis."[9] Copland and

---

[6] On James Copland see Peter Matheson: 'Copland, James,' from the *Dictionary of New Zealand Biography*, Te Ara – the Encyclopedia of New Zealand, updated 6-Jun-2013:
http://www.teara.govt.nz/en/biographies/2c32/copland-james (accessed 27 March, 2014). See also 'Dr. James Copland: First Goldfields Minister,' in *The Evangelical Presbyterian*, Vol. XI, No. 6, November, 1961, 36-38.

[7] Edinburgh: Andrew Elliot, 1874, vii+88pp.

[8] *The Evangelical Presbyterian*, Vol. XI, No. 6, November, 1961, 37.

[9] Peter Matheson: 'Copland, James,' from the *Dictionary of New Zealand Biography*, Te Ara – the Encyclopedia of New Zealand, updated 6-Jun-2013:

MacGregor were both unsuccessful in their applications as the theologically liberal Salmond was appointed in 1886. It seemed as though the authorities were not of a mind to appoint a 'conservative' applicant!

It was not long before issues of "modern theology" hit the shores of the Presbyterian Churches in New Zealand. In 1888 B. B. Warfield of Princeton Theological Seminary, in reviewing two pamphlets recently published in Dunedin, had occasion to remark that they brought news of the "outbreak of the 'New Theology' in the little Church of Otago and Southland, at the other side of the earth."[10] The pamphlets in question were written from entirely opposing points of view. One was by a William Salmond, D.D., Professor of Mental and Moral Philosophy at the University of Otago, and an ordained minister. The other – a reply to Salmond – was by James MacGregor. Salmond's subject was "The Reign of Grace." His thesis was well stated in the book's sub-title: "A discussion of the possibility of salvation for all men in this life or in the life to come."[11] In other words, Salmond was putting forward the heretical idea of Universalism as a possibility. This caused shock-waves in the Synod of Otago and Southland.

James MacGregor immediately took up the cudgels to counter the malignant teaching of the Professor. He wrote an answer in his *The Day of Salvation*. Again the sub-title accurately indicated his position: "[The Day of Salvation] obscured in a

---

http://www.teara.govt.nz/en/biographies/2c32/copland-james (accessed 27 March, 2014).

[10] *The Presbyterian Review*, Vol. IX, New York, 1888, 680. This was also printed under the title 'The New Theology in the Antipodes,' in the *Otago Daily Times*, Issue 8314, 15 October 1888, 4.

[11] William Salmond, *The Reign of Grace*, Dunedin, 1888, 64pp.

recent pamphlet on 'The Reign of Grace' "[12] One review of
the booklet was to maintain that "There is no man in the
Synod of Otago and Southland, or indeed within the bounds
of the Colonial Churches, more fit to grapple with a question
of Theology or to expound it with *curiosa felicitas* of genius than
the Minister of Oamaru."[13] B. B. Warfield, in his article, refers
favourably to MacGregor's pamphlet, writing that "it is a
thoroughly adequate reply to Salmond's arguments and a
satisfactory refutation of his position." Salmond wanted to
suggest "an extension of time during which the mercy of God
endures for repentant sinners." Shockingly, he knew that his
views could not be squared with the teaching of Christ, but
such an approach was to become not at all uncommon among
20th Century modern theologians. MacGregor was nothing if
he was not straight:

> 1. How could you, if you had a conscience, go on
> accepting wages for teaching as God's truth what
> you did not believe, but hated as the devil's lie? and
> 2. How could you, if you had a heart that was not
> of stone, remain silent when so many men were
> tortured with the thought of the finality of the
> present life, and not only remain silent, but really
> by your position, support the system of imposture
> that was tormenting them, and make a comfortable
> living by the fraud which was keeping them as in
> the pains of hell?

MacGregor answered Salmond point by point in his pamphlet.
He exposed Salmond's idea of God as a being reduced to a
scarcely personal benevolent force. Salmond thought his ideas

---

[12] James MacGregor, *The Day of Salvation*, Dunedin, 1888, 72pp.
[13] *Southland Times*, Issue 9885, 9 June, 1888, 3. Not all reviews were
favourable. See, for example, the review in *Otago Daily Times*, Issue 8199, 2
June, 1888, 5. The reviews are not attributed.

were a legitimate outworking of Calvinism. It was of course simple unbelief wrapped up in fine terms and sentiments. The case was a *cause célèbre* in the Synod which it seems did not deal properly with the matter. Initially the Dunedin Presbytery issued a censure before there was any trial and finally absolved him when there had been no retraction. In the end the Synod issued a *Pastoral Address* declaring "the doctrine of this Church in its published creed," as to "the finality of the present life in connection with the Gospel offer of salvation," to be, namely, "that the offer is to be made only in this life, and that at the day of judgement the wicked 'shall go away into everlasting punishment, but the righteous into life eternal.'"[14] This doctrine was therefore taken to be "true and Scriptural, and...believed, on the authority of the Scriptures and of the Son of God, by substantially the whole community of Christians upon earth in all ages of Church history."[15]

There were, however, pressures to modify the Church's creed, following the trends in Scotland. The idea of pursuing a Church union with the Presbyterian Church of New Zealand, and of making some modifications to the Confessional teaching, in line with those being proposed for the Scottish Churches, were put forward in the Synod of Otago and

---

[14] Presbyterian Church of Otago and Southland: Pastoral Address (issued November 2nd, 1888). Dunedin: Munro, Dunne & Co. 1888. 3.

[15] James MacGregor, *Presbyterians on Trial by their Principles*, Dunedin, 1890, 14. The relevant section of the *Confession of Faith* reads: "As Christ should have us to be certainly persuaded that there shall be a day of judgement, both to deter all men from sin, and for the greater consolation of the godly in their adversity; so will he have that day unknown to men, that they may shake off all carnal security, and be always watchful, because they know not at what hour the Lord will come; and may be ever prepared to say, Come, Lord Jesus, come quickly. Amen." (XXXIII:III).

Southland. James MacGregor never considered that proposals for revision of the *Westminster Confession* should be dismissed out of hand. However, he was utterly opposed to the weakening of the theological position of the Church and opposed enquiry into any such changes on the basis of "the unsuitableness of the time and the occasion, especially in connection with the lawless and disorderly proceedings of Dunedin Presbytery in the case of false doctrine, out of which, with ominous attendant circumstances, the movement had arisen."[16] Making things clearer is one thing; diminishing attainments in understanding of truth is another. He was clearly aware of what was behind so many of the arguments in his own Church. In one place he says this: "Dunedin Presbytery are not wholly original in their discovery (*overture*) that the Confession says (xxxi.4), – 'All Synods or Councils since the Apostles' times, whether general or particular, may err, and many have erred.' But the Presbytery," says MacGregor, "seem to have made a truly original application of this doctrine, to the effect of suggesting that the Confession is therefore *presumably in error* whenever a doubt or difficulty rises in connection with its teaching; *and* therefore, that the *formula* should be made indefinite, so as to fit into any doctrine that may occur to men."[17]

In the face of the evident weakening on the Confessional teaching, and the terms of ministerial subscription to that teaching, James MacGregor wrote two very strong pamphlets, *Freedom in the Truth under Shield of a Constitution of Government and*

---

[16] ibid., 5. The case referred to by MacGregor was of course that involving William Salmond.
[17] ibid., 5 (footnote).

of Doctrine, in accordance with the Word of God,[18] and *Blown in the Wind or Growing by the River? Presbyterians on Trial by Their Principles.*[19] These pamphlets were written in the context of debates within the Synod of Otago and Southland. In 1889 MacGregor was appointed to a Committee of enquiry with reference to doctrinal matters brought into question. However, his efforts to deal with such issues were met with resistance, no doubt because his views cut across the desire to modify certain teachings. By 1890 he had therefore felt he had to withdraw from the Committee. MacGregor is savage in his criticisms of the work of the Committees appointed by the Church in 1888 and 1889 to look into certain matters of doctrine thought to require explanation or qualification.[20]

MacGregor was clearly impatient with the Church and Committees in their apparent unwillingness really to grapple with doctrinal issues in question. Consequently, he made a sterling defence of the Confessional teaching in three areas raised: "*reprobation and preterition,* that of *the destiny of infants and others as spoken of in* Chap. X., 3, 4 *of the Confession,* and that of *the free Gospel offer of Salvation.*"[21] In MacGregor's view there was in connection with these matters misapprehension as to fact in relation to the actual teaching of the *Confession.* He endeavoured to clear these misapprehensions away one by one. The essential issue, he maintains, is *sovereign grace,* "the distinctive principle of the Calvinistic or Augustinian system

---

[18] Dunedin, 1889, 72pp.
[19] Dunedin, 1890, 40pp.
[20] Details of this are to be found in his *Presbyterians on Trial by their Principles,* pages 5 to 13 under "1. The Present Position of the Matter in this Church."
[21] ibid., 14.

of doctrine."[22] He wrote that "since the doubts and difficulties really impinge upon that principle, any yielding on the Church's part, in the direction of accommodating her creed to their pressure, would so far be an abandonment of her doctrinal basis of constitution in its principle, and, consequently, a virtual dissolution to her corporate existence as a society based on this creed."[23]

In relation to *Preterition and Reprobation* MacGregor wrote that *"objection to reprobation, or to preterition, really is objection to the sovereignty* of saving grace."[24] He defined reprobation in terms of the sinner being given over to his sin, and preterition in terms of sinners not being delivered from their sin and misery – being passed by. He made three points: (1) The dreadful thing is not the doctrine *per se*, but the reality involved; (2) What is dreadful in the thing is not the sovereignty of God but the hopeless ruin of the creatures; and, (3) "That sovereignty, which alone makes a Calvinism of reprobation, also alone makes the Calvinism of election."[25] After all, election and reprobation are two faces of the same sovereignty: God freely bestowing His love on whom He will in election, and sovereignly not bestowing them as He will upon the others. You cannot have one without the other, in the nature of the case. MacGregor used the illustration of Dives and his five apparently reprobate brothers, suggesting that if you reject the sovereignty of God operating in their case, how could you retain such sovereignty as a ground of

---

[22] ibid., 15.
[23] ibid., 15.
[24] ibid., 16.
[25] ibid., 17.

confidence as to the salvation of the 144,000 in Revelation 7? MacGregor deplored the inclination to sentimentalise the matter by effectively diminishing the holiness and justice of God working in the world, and at the same time underestimating the real sinfulness of sin. It was said that in the Presbyterian Church of Otago and Southland her ministers did not preach the distinctive Confessional doctrine of grace, so that either they did not believe it, or were afraid to preach it even though they did believe it. It was time, then, MacGregor maintained, to make a clear declaration on the Scriptural truth in relation to this Confessional teaching on election and reprobation, so that "by clear, unambiguous declaration of continued adherence to the Confession in the entirety of its Calvinistic system of doctrine:– in such a manner as to shew, that no ear-pleasing sound of double-meaning words about 'fatherhood' or 'love' shall be allowed, in the authorised teaching of this Church, to displace the evangelical doctrine of the sovereignty of that 'grace of God that bringeth salvation' (Titus ii., 11.)"[26]

In relation to *the destiny of infants and others as spoken of in the 10th Chapter of the Confession of Faith*, MacGregor countered the notion that the *Confession* teaches a doctrine of "infant damnation" in speaking of "elect infants." He made two main points: (1) any salvation of infants (or heathen) is a proof of the sovereign election of God; and (2) the sovereignty of grace is the only ground on which the salvation of either the adult heathen or infant Christian can be placed. MacGregor summarised the Confessional teaching as follows:

---

[26] ibid., 20.

The fact as to the teaching of the Confession in chapter x. 3, 4, is as follows:

1. The statement does not exclude the view that all who die in infancy are saved, nor express the view that adults cannot be saved if not reached with the outward means of salvation in the Word.

2. The statement bears expressly, that for such infants and adults there is salvation in the power of the sovereign grace of God, sanctifying and saving, in accordance with His good pleasure, by Christ through the Spirit, those whom He chooses.

3. The statement places the salvation of those infants and adults, as elsewhere the Confession places the salvation of all who shall be saved, on the foundation of the sovereign electing grace of God; and it strongly repels the view, that men can be saved otherwise than by redeeming grace in Christ, *e.g.*, by virtue of their natural morality and piety.

4. The use of the expression "elect infants" in Sec. 3 of the statement does not imply, that any who die in infancy are non-elect; and it is to be understood that the reference in the censure at Sec. 4 is simply to the view, that there can be human salvation otherwise than by the way of Christ's redemption.[27]

The third doctrinal issue addressed by James MacGregor is that of *the Free Gospel offer of Salvation.* The false notion he counters here is the idea that the free offer of the gospel – indiscriminately to elect and non-elect – cannot be believed along with the Confessional doctrine of sovereign grace. In his discussion at this point MacGregor covered much the same ground he did in his polemic against Amyraldianism in his 1870 pamphlet on *The Question of Principle now raised in the Free*

---

[27] ibid., 22-23.

Church specially regarding the Atonement, as described in the
chapter on the Union Controversy above. He made three
main points: (1) The indiscriminate free Gospel offer to elect
and non-elect is certainly taught in the *Confession,* most notably
in the chapter on "God's Covenant with man."[28] (2) How it is
possible for God sincerely to offer all sinners a salvation
which He purposes to bestow on only some, the *Confession*
makes no endeavour to explain, any more than it seeks to
explain how all men can be sincerely commanded to keep the
moral law, whilst to only some He gives a new heart and a
right spirit. Whilst some such things cannot be understood or
reconciled, nonetheless we can believe that they must be
compatible somehow. "According to God's own Word in
Christ (*e.g.,* Mat. xx.16; xxii.14), the general calling and the
special choosing, on the part of God the Saviour, both alike
are facts in the system of our salvation by grace,"[29] (3) The
warrant for the free Gospel offer is simply the declared will of
God, commanding all men everywhere to repent. The
warranting ground is not some general grace, or a wistfulness
on the part of God that all should be saved, but which does
not *secure* the salvation of any. There can be no other warrant
than the will of God, His mere good pleasure. Wrote
MacGregor: "it is among communities addressed on the
footing of the sovereignty of grace that the gospel, in the
conversion of sinners as well as upbuilding of believers, has
most signally had free course and been glorified through the
ages."[30]

---

[28] *Westminster Confession of Faith,* Chapter VII:III.
[29] James MacGregor, *Presbyterians on Trial by their Principles,* 24.
[30] ibid., 28.

Notwithstanding his generally robust position on retaining the Confession as it was, when it was later proposed in the Synod of Otago and Southland at a meeting held in October 1892, that the Synod should accept the Free Church Declaratory Act of 1892 MacGregor expressed himself in the Synod as "perfectly satisfied with the Declaratory Act of the Free Church" but felt it only fair that it be sent down for wider discussion and opinion before the Synod settled the issue. However, it was finally moved and accepted that the Synod "Adopt the recommendation of the committee and send down the Declaratory Act of the Free Church to the Presbyteries and kirk sessions with a view to its adoption by the synod."[31]

Whilst the Free Church Declaratory Act did not alter the *Confession of Faith* its tenor was to loosen the distinctive aspect of the sovereignty of grace and establish vagueness by introducing the concept of points that did not enter into the substance of the Reformed Faith. The fact that these points were undefined was, potentially, a doctrinally destructive element in the Act.[32] It was a disappointing aspect of this issue that a man of MacGregor's acumen and insight, and obvious attachment to the "whole doctrine of the Confession," did not discern such evident weaknesses – and dangers – in the Free Church Act.

---

[31] *Otago Daily Times*, Issue 9570, 28 October 1892, 4.

[32] The clause in question read: "That while diversity of opinion is recognised in this Church on such points in the Confession as do not enter into the substance of the Reformed Faith therein set forth, the Church retains full authority to determine, in any case which may arise, what points fall within this description, and thus to guard against any abuse of this liberty to the detriment of sound doctrine, or to the injury of her unity and peace."

In closing his pamphlet *Presbyterians on Trial by their Principles*, MacGregor provided a strong defence of the merits of the *Westminster Confession*. "The Confession," he wrote, "is simply Calvinism, with what otherwise may be called the commonplaces of Christian teaching exhibited in a manner of confessedly unsurpassed excellence."[33] Apart from some statements in relation to the Civil Magistrate, there is "nothing in this whole complexity of detailed articulations that occasions perplexity where men are agreed upon the substance of the whole: the Calvinism, in straightforward clear simplicity, is 'all in the whole, and all in every part'; so that a real Calvinist in going into this and that detail, finds only cause for satisfaction on account of the masterly manner in which the substance of doctrine believed by him is here worked out into the detailed application."[34] In MacGregor's view it is the greatest of the Calvinistic creeds, "the greatest of all symbolic monuments of that *sovereign love* of God, which is the distinctive principle of the Calvinistic evangelism of doctrinal system."[35] It is a guarding fence of strength in relation to truth, like the mountains round about Jerusalem. It seemed clear to James MacGregor that any departure from the Confessional system and teaching would require to be met with the resistance. Whilst not a perfect creed, nor one which might not be reshaped, it was nonetheless not something to be tampered with unless there were good reasons, and certainly not out of a desire to evade the truths it so magnificently expounds.

---

[33] James MacGregor, *Presbyterians on Trial by their Principles*, 29.
[34] ibid., 29.
[35] ibid., 32.

At least in MacGregor's time, moves to alter the doctrine of the *Confession* and the ministerial subscription to it were resisted, probably in large measure due to the weight of the arguments he brought to bear on these matters in his pamphlets defensive of the full-orbed doctrines of sovereign grace.

James MacGregor

13

DEFENDER OF THE FAITH

In a review of James MacGregor's *Studies in the History of Christian Apologetics* (1894) Marcus Dods was to characterise the author's approach in this way:

> It is a healthy and vigorous – perhaps superabundantly vigorous – treatise. Dr. Macgregor thinks poorly of gladiators as fighting men in serious warfare, but he constantly appears to his reader as a gladiator, ready with his weapons, a trained and skilled fighter, delighting in the game, and a shade ruthless in antagonism.[1]

No doubt the reference to ruthlessness in antagonism arises from the fact that in the book in question MacGregor takes such serious issue with positions with which the reviewer would have had sympathy!

In his later years, no doubt burdened by the increasing necessity for the defence of the Faith, James MacGregor devoted himself to a series of books on Christian Apologetics. In the last four years of his life he produced three massive tomes on such themes. It is clear that he "continued to read widely in addition to his parish duties and the three volumes he wrote on apologetics were a remarkable achievement for a busy parish minister."[2]

---

[1] *The Expositor*, Fourth Series, Volume X. London, 1894, 466.
[2] Ian Breward, "Lloyd Geering and James MacGregor," in James Veitch (Editor), *Faith in an Age of Turmoil*, London, 1990, 193.

The first of these volumes on apologetics was published by T. & T. Clark in 1891. In some ways it was MacGregor's *magnum opus*. The full title was, *The Apology of the Christian Religion Historically Regarded with Reference to Supernatural Revelation and Redemption*. It was a weighty volume of 544 pages. After an Introductory survey of 21 pages, the volume is divided into two Books, the first (25-202) covering "The Religion at Work in the Second Century", and the second (203-544) covering "The External Evidences of the Religion." In a review of the book the *Expository Times* recognises the obvious, namely, that "it is a great claim which Dr Macgregor makes by the title of his new book." It does go on to say, however, flatteringly, that the author "has the ability (shall we say genius?) to entitle him to range alongside the greatest of the Christian Apologists."[3] The reviewer suggests that the book does reach the magnificent claim which its title makes for it.

In this volume MacGregor early stated his presuppositions. MacGregor writes from within the context of critical movements in Biblical studies. What is the core issue? Wrote MacGregor: "While on the surface there is cavilling or debating about particulars of the Bible religion and its documents, the question really is of supernaturalism in general, and the real opponent is atheistic naturalism, – a quintessential worldliness of metaphysic, perhaps in gown and bands, masquerading under forms of historical induction and literary judgement."[4] The religion presented by MacGregor is

---

[3] At the Literary Table. The Books of the Month. *The Expository Times*. Vol. III, Oct., 1891 – Sept., 1892, 136.

[4] James MacGregor, *The Apology of the Christian Religion*, Edinburgh 1891, 19.

one of "all-pervasive thorough-going supernaturalism." He expressed his presuppositions thus:

> The Church is a new kingdom of God among men, wherein He dwells in a supernatural Presence that is realised through ordinances. "God is light;" and there is a coming righteous judgment of all men according to their works. In eternity, "the door is shut:" but now, repentance and forgiveness of sins are to be preached to all nations in the name of Christ; with certification, that there is no other name under heaven, given among men, whereby we may be saved. The Bible is an oracular Book, of which the primary author is the Holy Ghost who moved the holy men of God that wrote it: so that the Scripture cannot be broken, because what "is written" is God's word. Christ is God incarnate. He was conceived in a virgin's womb, and is risen from the dead. Atonement in Him is God's provision of reconciliation on a righteous way of peace with guilty sinners, namely, the way of expiatory sacrifice, provided by the sovereign redeeming love of God, to satisfy His justice offended by their sin. Regeneration is new creation, by sovereignly efficacious grace of the Divine Spirit. Justification is free pardon and acceptance, received by faith as a pure and simple gift of God's mercy, and bestowed by Him on the ground of His own righteousness in Christ. Sin is sinful. It is not natural evil merely, but distinctively moral evil. It brings guilt on the sinner, placing him under condemnation; and constitutes in him a spiritual condition of impotency in pollution. God hates it in His holiness, and in His rectoral justice punishes it with death. The race of man is fallen into an inheritance of corruption and of guilt; so that all men are by nature children of wrath, born slaves of sin. Deliverance is possible only through

sovereignty of divine redeeming mercy. In order to man's redemption, incarnation is assumption of complete manhood by a person who is truly God. In the unity of Godhead there be three Persons. The Holy Ghost is a distinct person; who, proceeding from the Father and the Son, works in men graciously, quickening and sanctifying the redeemed of Christ, the elect of God. Creation is the origination, mediately or immediately, of all things in the universe by free action of God's will. Providence is His ruling all their action and sustaining them all in being. Special providence is His directing the course of events in the world to accomplishment of His purposes toward, and in connection with the Church. Miracle is extraordinary providence, exhibiting "the finger of God." Prophecy is supernatural communication of His mind. In prediction of the incalculable, it is a miracle of wisdom; so as to be, like miracle of power, an evidential wonder or attesting "seal." Prayer is "asking" from "Our Father who is in heaven."[5]

For the vindication of the Christian religion MacGregor relied upon two main things: (1) On what he calls "internal evidence," that is to say, the evidence from its widespread diffusion in the world. In view of the ostensibly feeble beginning how could you account for its spread apart from the truth of it and the reality of the work of God in it? (2) On what he calls "direct external evidence," that is to say, the evidence in open court, as it were, demonstrable in relation to its claims.

---

[5] James MacGregor, *The Apology of the Christian Religion*, Edinburgh, 1891, 20-21.

His work is a sterling defence of the Christian religion. It is written from the point of view of one who believed in historic orthodoxy (Calvinism). His approach is based squarely on the fact of the supernatural, the reality of the miraculous, and in particular of the resurrection of Christ. These provide, for MacGregor, abundant attestation of the truth of historic Christianity. He accepts of course the authority of Biblical revelation and its historical nature. It is utterly trustworthy. He is particularly concerned to establish the importance of the Old Testament. It is clear that he feels that this has been undermined somewhat by the trends in Old Testament criticism then current. In one place he wrote, "It therefore is well that we should be on our guard against that disposition to ignore the Old Testament;" and he went on to write that "To ignore the Old Testament is to exclude from view a very important evidence of the divinity of the New Testament religion."[6] "Regarding the New Testament religion," wrote MacGregor, "the root question of Apologetic in our day is as to the supernatural."[7] Concerning the actions of the Apostles he wrote in one place that "They are not mere authors of a new philosophy or morality of nature, nor merely the publishers of a new edition of the religion of nature; they are *ministers* of a new supernatural revelation; they are heralds proclaiming the free gift of a supernatural redemption from the sovereign grace of God to a ruined race of men. And, correspondingly, as to the mainspring, fountain, sunrise of all the movements thus begun, they are *witnesses* of the historical

---

[6] ibid., 418.
[7] ibid., 419.

Christ, in the historical reality of His resurrection as 'manifestation of His glory.' "[8]

MacGregor's approach is essentially a traditional evidentialist one. It is interesting that in a review of this volume by William Brenton Greene, Jr, of Princeton Theological Seminary, Greene points out how different the approach of MacGregor is to a volume produced around the same time by Professor A. B. Bruce of the Glasgow Free Church College.[9] Bruce was inclined to accommodate to the then current critical positions, whereas MacGregor wrote "in the spirit of strong, I had almost said bitter, and yet most intelligent opposition to the Higher Criticism."[10] The evaluation of this book by Greene – no mean judge – is worth noting: "The style of the work is not perfect. If there were more periodic sentences the book would read more easily. Nevertheless, it is, in the main, clear to him who thinks; it is enriched with a wealth of varied learning; it abounds in comparisons as vigorous as they are original."[11] Although an original piece of work it is doubtless too wordy to be popular and tended, like his other volumes, to sink into unfortunate obscurity.

The second volume of the trilogy was *The Revelation and the Record. Essays on Matters of Previous Question in the Proof of Christianity.* This was published by T. & T. Clark a couple of years after the first volume. The subjects dealt with in this volume are "(1) relatively to Revelation, the *supernatural*, – as

---

[8] ibid., 322.
[9] *Apologetics; or, Christianity Defensively Stated*, Edinburgh, 1892.
[10] *The Presbyterian and Reformed Review*, Vol. V, 1894, 110-111.
[11] ibid.

involved in the system of things, and constitution of man, the fact of religion, – as implied in the internal evidence of Christianity and the Bible, – and as operative in the divine inspiration of Scripture; (2) relatively to Record, *the New testament canon*, or the title of the Scriptures now received on that canon to be held as genuine writings of apostles and their authorised associates."[12] MacGregor's position is clearly conservative. Indeed, a review in *The Expository Times* stated that "the writer's attitude is distinctly conservative throughout, but he has the ability to make even that which we now consider the extreme of conservatism seem not only the most reasonable, but the only possible position."[13] At that time of course theories of inspiration were being influenced by literary criticism. MacGregor persisted in deducing his doctrine of inspiration from the Scriptures themselves as ultimately deriving from divine authorship. "It was Macgreggor's (*sic*) conviction," says H. D. McDonald, "that the supernaturalism of the Bible's inspiration and the divinity of its authorship are one and the same reality."[14] MacGregor went out of his way to state his belief in verbal inspiration. There is no other type of inspiration which has any significance or permanent reality: "Those who imagine that there can be an inspiration of Scripture that is *not* a 'verbal' inspiration may have some notion of divine 'ideas' floating in the air, like 'songs without words,' when men are talking like Moses and Elias on the

---

[12] James MacGregor, *Studies in the History of Christian Apologetics*, Edinburgh, 1894, 3.

[13] At the Literary Table, *The Expository Times*, Vol. V, Oct. 1893 – Sept., 1894, 84.

[14] H. D. McDonald, *Theories of Revelation. An Historical Study 1860-1960*, London, 1963, 271.

Mount of Transfiguration."[15] "It is the *Scripture* that is
inspired," wrote MacGregor, "the human writer is *employed* in
producing it."[16]

The third volume of the trilogy was just finished shortly
before his death in 1894. It constitutes *Studies in the History of
Christian Apologetics: New Testament and Post Apostolic.* In this
volume MacGregor opens up the subject again in two
sections. The first deals with the New Testament in which he
shows the apologetic approach successively in the ministries
of Christ and of the Apostles. The second deals with post-
Apostolic period of apologetics, with reference to what he
calls the *Primitive* period, that is to say from 130 A.D. to the
close of the sixteenth century, and then the *Modern* period,
from the close of the sixteenth century. It is in this last
section that MacGregor dealt with the then controversial
matters of Old Testament Criticism. It is evident from his
sharp critique of the Higher Critics such as Graf, Keunen,
Wellhausen and S. R. Driver, and his favourable citations from
such writers as those of the Princeton School, William Henry
Green and Geerhardus Vos, and Professor James Robertson
of Glasgow, just where he stood on these contentious issues.[17]
MacGregor was, indeed, a rigorous critic of the 'destructive'
Critics. He was still, however, somewhat naïve about the work
and influence of A. B. Davidson[18] and William Robertson

[15] James MacGregor, *The Revelation and the Record*, Edinburgh, 1893, 109.
[16] ibid., 96 (footnote).
[17] MacGregor acknowledges his indebtedness to the conservative
American scholars in his, *Studies in the History of Christian Apologetics*,
Edinburgh, 1894, 279-281. His appreciation of the work of James
Robertson is found in pages 332 to 335 of that same work.
[18] ibid., 278.

Smith.[19] However, B. B. Warfield was to comment with reference to this work, and in particular that part of it dealing with the modern issues, that the subject was "treated with ability and grasp, with wide knowledge and above all with marked independence." He went on to say that the reader will "feel himself in the hands of a master at every step, will be allowed no moment of drowsiness in the whole progress of the discussion, and will lay down the volumes with the conviction that they embodied a substantial contribution to the apologetical literature of our times."[20]

His three later works on apologetics constitute for James MacGregor a considerable achievement. It is probably true to say that although Warfield would suggest that "the three volumes may well stand as his honourable monument, as they will, wherever they are read, powerfully advance the cause he had at heart,"[21] yet it would have to be recognised that they had little impact on the Christian world of his own day. The method he adopted is not beyond criticism. Although the works display great learning, real earnestness and a pervasive Biblical soundness in many respects, the approach may be considered rather too rationalistic. MacGregor appeared to think – as many did in those days – that an unfolding of various evidences for Christian faith would be persuasive to any right-thinking person. But the extensive effects of sin in the lives of fallen people ensure an inability to grasp even the most persuasive pleadings from what the Christian believer

---

[19] ibid., 337-338.
[20] *The Presbyterian and Reformed Review*, Philadelphia, Vol. VIII, 1897, 772-773.
[21] ibid., 773.

sees as obviously true. Fallen man, alas, will always find ways of interpreting 'facts' in a way that squares with his anti-theistic bias or perverse presuppositions.

Increasingly in the 20th Century the presentation of what were considered as reasonable evidences supportive of Christianity were considered to be invalidated by a materialistic view of phenomena in the world. The darkness of people's minds by nature leaves them incapable of assessing 'facts' in creation and in the Word aright. A Christian epistemology is the only valid outlook on faith and life. The unbeliever, however, will best be challenged at the level of his anti-theistic presuppositions, and that inevitably he holds the truth in unrighteousness (Romans 1:18). The best and most reasonable arguments will not prevail with fallen man. What will prevail is the work of the Spirit to enlighten and convict that "by faith we understand that the worlds were framed by the word of God, so that the things which are seen were not made of things which are visible" (Hebrews 11:3). This of course James MacGregor well understood. "Paul by and by (1 Cor. ii.)," he wrote in his *Apology of the Christian Religion*, "will be able to say, from experimenting among mankind, that the clearest and fullest external evidence is unavailing, unless God Almighty, along with outward light, give the inward gift of sight. It is important that the future apostles should be early made to know this; so that from the outset they may depend only on that power (Acts i.8) from on high, and may proceed upon the view and feeling (1 Cor. iii.6) that all real success has to come, not from wisdom, power, or authority of theirs, but only from the Spirit of the Lord of Hosts."[22]

James MacGregor was a voice against the Critics in his day and as such placed himself within that body of witnesses who stood for the utter trustworthiness and complete inspiration of the canon of Scripture in a day which saw widespread defection from such positions in the Churches. The volumes which comprise his trilogy on apologetics clearly did not have a wide circulation. The present writer was able in 1968 to obtain the first and third of these volumes in their original form new from T. & T. Clark's offices in 38 George Street, Edinburgh. Yet they are not easily obtained on the second-hand market. It is true to say, however, that they still repay study and leave the distinct impression of representing an earnest desire to defend the faith as historically understood in an age of growing scepticism and unbelief.[23]

---

[22] James MacGregor, *The Apology of the Christian Religion*, Edinburgh, 1891, 402.

[23] For a more recent, if somewhat limited, discussion of MacGregor's apologetics see the essay of Ian Breward, "Lloyd Geering and James MacGregor: Two New Zealand Apologists," in the volume *Faith in an Age of Turmoil. Essays in honour of Lloyd Geering*. Edited by James Veitch. London, 1990, pp190-202.

14

FAMILY MATTERS

James and Grace MacGregor in all were blessed with ten children. The first two of them – Georgina and Duncan – were born in Barry. Sadly, both these children became afflicted with tuberculosis and died in Edinburgh in their teens – Georgina ('Nina') in 1874, aged 16, and Duncan ('Dutta') in 1878 aged 18. The MacGregors' second son was named William Cunningham after his father's Theological professor at New College.

William ('Willie') was born in Paisley in 1862 and educated at George Watson's College in Edinburgh, and the University of Edinburgh, where he started a law degree which, however, he did not complete before he emigrated with the family from Scotland to New Zealand in 1881. He transferred, however, to Otago University where he passed his final law examinations in 1883. An exceedingly bright student, that year he received the Canterbury Law Society's gold medal for his work. He was to become an outstandingly successful lawyer. But in his youth William was quite a sportsman, playing cricket for the Carisbrook Club (Dunedin), and rugby for the Dunedin Club. In 1898-99 he was champion of the Otago Golf Club.[1]

---

[1] For Biographical details of William Cunningham MacGregor see G. H. Scholefield (Editor), *A Dictionary of New Zealand Biography*, Volume II (M-Addenda). Wellington: Department of Internal Affairs, 1940, 17-18. [See http://www.nzhistory.net.nz/files/documents/dnzb-1940/scholefield-

William married Dora Louisa Harris, daughter of G. W.
Harris of Mount Gambier, South Australia, in 1902. From the
marriage there were three children: Helen, Duncan and Cecil.
William practised law in Dunedin from 1890 to 1920 and was
President of the Otago Law Society in 1898. In 1903 he
became a partner in the firm of Smith, MacGregor and
Sinclair. For many years he was a legal advisor to the Dunedin
City Council and in 1914 became Crown Prosecutor for the
Otago District, taking silk that same year. Appointed Solicitor-
General of New Zealand in 1920 William, whilst in control of
the Crown Law Office, had to assume most of the duties of
the Attorney-General, Sir Frances Bell, during the latter's
absence in Geneva. In 1923 he became a judge of the
Supreme Court from which he retired in 1934.

William made contributions from time to time to the press
and periodicals and was responsible for two important studies:
Ideals of Empire[2] and *Scottish Law at the Antipodes.*[3] He did not
enjoy a long retirement, passing away suddenly on 26th August,
1934, whilst in London on a visit to his son and daughter,
Duncan and Helen.[4]

Duncan Bernays MacGregor, William and Dora's eldest
son, became a minister in the Scottish Episcopal Church.
Having graduated from the University of New Zealand in

---

dnzb-v2.pdf (accessed 6th January, 2006)]. See also, *Who's Who New Zealand*, 1924, 1932.
[2] Dunedin: *Otago Daily Times*, 1908. This is described as *"a public lecture delivered…at the Athenaeum, Dunedin, on Tuesday 5th May 1908"*. It was produced in a book format.
[3] Edinburgh: The (Law) Review, 1925, pp212-218. This was an excerpt from *The Judicial Review*, v. 37, no. 3 (Sept. 1925).
[4] *The Evening Post* [Wellington, NZ], Volume CXVIII, Issue 49, 27 August 1934, p10.

1923, Duncan subsequently went up to Westcott House, Cambridge, to study (as the Episcopalians say) for 'Holy Orders.' He completed studies in Cambridge in 1929 and became Curate in several English Parishes, though he did return briefly to the Wellington Diocese in 1932. In 1938, however, Duncan moved to Lochgilphead in Argyll where he served as Rector until 1945, moving then to Pittenweem in Fife (1945-51). Subsequently he moved back south as Vicar at Marton and Gate Burton (Lincolnshire, 1951-53) and then St Matthew's, Burnley (Lancashire, 1954-55). The remainder of Duncan's ministry was spent in Scotland, at Walkerburn (1956) and South Queensferry (1956-60). In 1958 Duncan produced a popular 'apologia' for the Scottish Episcopal Church entitled *Scottish and Anglican*, a 29-page work which was No. 3 in a series of booklets published by his Church. Needless-to-say it betrays a very different perspective from that of his Presbyterian grandfather! Duncan retired in 1960 and passed away three years later. A son, Andrew Duncan John MacGregor was born in 1936 and became a naval architect. He also had a daughter, Alison.[5]

James and Grace MacGregors' third, son, James ('Jamie'), was also born in Paisley (1863). James also was stricken by Tuberculosis and it was particularly on account of his poor health that the move to New Zealand was contemplated and undertaken. Sadly, on the one-hundred-day voyage on the

---

[5] For details of Duncan MacGregor see David M. Bertie, *Scottish Episcopal Clergy 1689-2000*, Edinburgh, 2000, 347. The entry for Duncan MacGregor only mentions the one son, Andrew, and makes no reference to a daughter. How Duncan became an *Episcopal* clergyman given the strong Presbyterian background is unknown. Whether he would be classed as an evangelical is also unknown.

Jessie Readman out to New Zealand he passed away on the ship. His second son, William, and the six younger daughters all arrived safely. Except the oldest surviving daughter, Helen, they would all live into their seventies, and three of them into their nineties!

James MacGregor, who was quite a poet, was to compose some verse as a tribute – a beautiful one it must be said – to the little ones "gone before." It was printed in the *Oamaru Mail* under the title "Of Such":

> Blest light of life! That sayest, "before, not lost,"
> At Thy redeemed immortals' destination
> Arrive safe in bliss; – that we, if tossed
> In stormy darkness, "working out salvation,"
> May trust our loved ones to Thy "gone before,"
> And hope to meet them shining at heaven's door.[6]

The oldest surviving daughter, Helen ('Nellie'), was born in Paisley on 26th May, 1865. Helen devoted her life to missionary service in India. She was obviously very close to her father, not only in bonds of family affection, but also by bonds of Christian love. A letter to her from her father, written by him whilst he was away from home on a preaching trip shortly after arriving in New Zealand, provides a lovely insight into their relationship and family life in general in the MacGregor household:

Mr Cameron's Church
5th January 1882

My Dear Nellie,
I am well pleased to see that you and Ada [younger sister Agnes] are taking pains to write well. I hope you will both hold on until you have got a formed good hand. The plan I suggested would, I think,

---

[6] *Oamaru Mail*, Monday, October 8, 1894.

be a good one:– viz., that you should select some fine piece of poetry – say one of Milton's sonnets – and write it as if you were contending for a prize in writing. The poetry would at the same time be fixing itself on your memory and forming your taste, and you could cross-question one another on the grammar, logic and rhetoric. I gave out a copy of the *Paradise Lost* which has explanatory notes. I wish that regularly, at a fixed time, there should be a section read aloud and the explanatory notes consulted for the meaning of obscure passages. Milton's elaborate blank verse is one of the best means of higher study on English; and a very good exercise to turn the poetry completely into prose. I wish you now to be turning over in your mind, with a view to setting your habits, the question, how best to set about systematic study, especially in the lines on which you have already entered. With assistance you can get at home, you among yourselves can, by simply taking pains at fixed times, do much by way, not only of retaining what you have, but of indefinitely extending your attainments. The younger children, too, ought to be getting under way, with special reference to Kathie, for instance. I do not think there is pressing need of haste in getting up much knowledge: what I think more important at present is, the formation of a habit of orderly work, especially at tasks which are not fascinating in themselves – avoiding overstrain.

I have a deepening sense of the importance of *systematic* study of Bible History and doctrine. Perhaps for the history a good enough method is that which you have been practising on Sabbath afternoons – taking a leading biography, with the relative maps. That will naturally and easily draw in along with itself the connected general history and antiquities – such as you find in Kitto's *Illustrated Bible*. But especially for your seniors – I should like a connected study of the main doctrines of Christianity. Perhaps the best method of this would be examining one another on the meaning of the *Catechism* questions as answered by the little ones, and on the Bible evidence for the doctrines thus conversed about. I am led to this line of remark, partly by what I have been observing in connection with weekday and Sabbath day school work. It is clear to me that, even in order to profit duly by the public instructions at Church, people must early get into the habit of *personally* thinking and inquiring on the ground of Scripture. I am told that in this colony we will be astonished by the rapidity with which you all, if you live, shall shoot up into women. And it is a dreadful want in a woman's education not to be an intelligent student of Bible history and doctrine, knowing much and therefore hungering for more. To any one in mature life, it is the greatest blessing under heaven to be a habitual student, *with relish*, of the real contents of Scripture; and the relish for this habitual study is the reward of what at first is but a custom, or repetition of action by so many exertions of will. In this case the true ultimate source of relish, custom, habit is set forth in Jno. 15:1 etc.

At the child's funeral yesterday I found another of those endless coincidences which make my work here so interesting. Having preached on Sabbath about the Church membership of infants, I found I had forgotten to give the following illustration of the doctrine: In Balquhidder long ago I was impressed with what was contributed in a Gaelic (?) hymn by one Mary Stuart, viz. an address from a child in heaven for consolation of its bereaved parents on earth; and last winter I was delighted to find that hymn among the "Spiritual Songs" (Gaelic?) of the late Mr Peter Grant of Grantown in Strathspey. Well, at the funeral was a MacGregor from Badenoch and he told me today, the baby's mother (married to an Englishman) is from Grantown in Strathspey, *and* a cousin of the Grants (one, the Rev. Wm. Grant) I knew in Edinburgh, who are children of that Peter Grant. Something like this, but not so interesting, occurred in Taieri. Through a mistake of mine I discovered that Mrs _____ is a niece of the late Hugh McLauchlan of Aberdeen, a famous scholar who edited an edition of Ossian [?] in Gaelic, the edition which was published and circulated gratuitously (1818) by Sir John Murray MacGregor Bart.

Mr and Mrs Cameron have suggested a ride to Kaiapoi, where one can see a woollen factory. I have thankfully declined for two reasons:– (1) I don't want to see a woollen factory, I really would rather not. You perceive, I have seen plenty of woollen factories though Canterbury people have not; and the *fact* of there being one at Kaiapoi, though interesting, is learned by me here as well as if I were to take the 20 miles journey (going and coming). By the way, I had learned this fact in the forenoon, from a shopman in whose window I had seen woollen cloth marked as "Kaiapoi." The rise of such factories, as Kaiapoi and Mosgiel, is fateful to such a colony as this with wool so cheap and cloth so dear. In the 2nd place, I wanted to be alone. I said this plainly, but courteously; explaining that, with running so much up and down the world, I have little opportunity for real solitude, and that I feel much need of it ever since Dutta's death [his first son, Duncan], a need of which the feeling is deeper since James'.

It is a good thing for me to have pleasure in this taking you and the others into my solitude when the mood is upon me. Absolute solitude is fit only for a beast or for a god (see Bacon's *Essay on Friendship*). But in order to the solitude that is fit for a man his companionship must be of his own choosing, and at his discretion to begin or end. Now your society is that which I prefer to all others and I call you in here, and dismiss you, without so much as a word spoken, by a simple act of will. I find that Dutta and James are never company to me in the way that baby was in Mary Stuart's contribution.

I had thought of requesting Dr or Mrs Murdoch (née Blackie) to meet me at Ashburton Station, where the train stops for a few minutes. But I have made up my mind against this, as being on my part too imperial in manner, and presupposing on theirs a species and degree of warmth of which I have no certainty.

I know that I can purchase collars here if I need. But it is not for advice to that effect that I sent in my need, from a house containing ten pairs of female hands, not one of which makes a farthing to support the household. What I wanted was, to save the great waste of money resulting from purchasing here what can well be otherwise provided. To give out things to wash here is not so simple and easy *for me* as it may appear to some, and might be more costly than to purchase new one's downright.

Your wandering
Père-ambulator

It appears that Helen MacGregor was first encouraged to think of mission work in India as a result of an appeal made for workers by a Mrs Longhurst of the Church of Scotland Zenana Mission, Madras, on a visit to Otago and Southland in

1892. A standard history of the Presbyterian Church in New
Zealand records that, "In 1892, in response to an appeal for
workers from the Church of Scotland Women's Mission at
Madras, Miss Helen MacGregor had been sent out, thus
becoming the first Presbyterian missionary to India from New
Zealand."[7] Helen MacGregor in point of fact went out in
1893.[8] Initially she was engaged in school work but ill health
forced her to return to New Zealand for a period "under the
double strain of climate and language study."[9]

In 1900, however, Helen returned on the complete
restoration of her health. This time, however, she applied
through the Otago Presbyterian Women's Missionary Union,
an organisation which had been formed in 1897 "to further
among the women of the Church missions in the New
Hebrides and among the Chinese resident within the bound
and to undertake the work of Mission Aid Association and of
the Women's Mission to Madras."[10]

On 23rd November 1899 a proposal was made by that
Union to the Free Church of Scotland Women's Foreign
Missionary Society that Miss Helen MacGregor be appointed
an agent of the Free Church of Scotland for the India mission
field. On 24th January 1900 a letter of acceptance of the
proposal came from the Rev. William Stevenson, Secretary of
the Women's Foreign Missionary Society of the Free Church

---

[7] John Rawson Elder, *The History of the Presbyterian Church of New Zealand
1840-1940*, Christchurch 1940, 292. Cf. William Ewing (Editor), *Annals of
the Free Church of Scotland, 1843-1900*. Vol. I. Edinburgh, 1914, 74.
[8] John Collie, *The Story of the Otago Free Church Settlement 1848-1948*,
Dunedin 1949(?), 270.
[9] Elder, op. cit., 314.
[10] Collie, op. cit., 271.

in Scotland. The arrangement was that the New Zealand Church would pay half the salary and the Free Church the other half. This would have been greatly approved by her late father, who in 1874 in an article in *The Family Treasury*, made such a plea for India mission work. Subsequently to the union of the Free and United Presbyterian Churches in October 1900, the mission in which she was employed came under the auspices of the United Free Church of Scotland.

It was reported in 1902 that her knowledge of Tamil had enabled her to start work in Madras at once, and that she had kept well since returning in 1900. The Report for 1904 stated that the Assembly of the Presbyterian Church of New Zealand had taken responsibility for her full salary, though three years later it was noted that they reduced their contribution back to 50% (presumably the United Free Church came in again with the other half). In 1909 the New Zealand Church opened its own Indian field in the Punjab and it was reported that Helen MacGregor would be left wholly to the United Free Church of Scotland. It appears that she retired from mission service in 1917, whereupon she served for some five months at a Home Mission work in Eketahuna within the Wairarapa Presbytery of the Presbyterian Church in New Zealand. She then lived at 41 Inglis Street, Seatoun, near Dunedin, with her two unmarried sisters, Agnes and Grace, until her death in 1933.

Both Agnes ('Ada') and Grace were to live into their nineties. Agnes passed way in 1962 and Grace the following year. Agnes is particularly noteworthy in New Zealand folklore through the *Diary* that she wrote as a young girl chronicling the journey to New Zealand on the *Jessie Readman* in 1881 and subsequent life in the MacGregor family in Dunedin and Oamaru. In 1897 she was appointed 'Letter Secretary' of the Presbyterian Women's Missionary Union at its first meeting.[11] Grace became a teacher, but after some years in teaching, she retired to offer herself for Home Mission work in Otira, Canterbury, in 1921. She worked among women and children, but resigned in 1923 on grounds of ill health. She did, however, eventually live into her nineties.

Helen MacGregor was quite influential in the experience of the oldest daughter of her younger sister, Catherine McLean MacGregor, who was born in Edinburgh on 16th August, 1870.[12] Catherine ('Cathie') married William Alexander Patterson on 16th February, 1898. Their first daughter, Grace Marion, was born in Wellington on 17th May 1899. It is said of her that as a student at Victoria University College she "was involved in questioning and protest to the extent that her church connection became marginal." She must have had a change of heart, however, and through her Aunt Helen's influence and the challenge at a student conference about the need for talented people to offer their skill to meet the desperate social, educational and medical needs in India, she offered herself for mission work there. This was to be her life's work. In 1926 she was ready to go to Jagadhri, India, but was turned down by the New Zealand Presbyterian Church Foreign Missions Committee on health

---

[11] ibid., 271.

[12] In various on-line ancestral records Catherine's name is given as Katherine Maclean MacGregor. However, the Scottish birth records clearly record her name as *Catherine McLean* MacGregor. It is possible that this is a scribal error and that the parents intended Katherine with a 'K'! However, the birth certificate has 'C'.

grounds. Undeterred she later applied to the Church of Scotland. Though her doctor gave her a certificate for a hill station only, this was sufficient for the Church of Scotland which, on receiving her medical certificate, wired her back with the message: "Come at once." Grace sailed for India on Friday, 13th April 1928, no doubt to the delight of her Aunt Helen. She subsequently served the Lord and the Church conscientiously in educational work, from which she finally retired back to Khandallah in December 1962. In an Obituary after her death on 5th January 1996 we read that following her retirement from the mission field "She continued her active life enjoying meeting people, listening to music, going to the beach, swimming, attending talks and seminars especially those related to India or the church. She loved her God and served Him well throughout her life, and her Church gives thanks to God for her faithful dedicated service."

One of Grace Patterson's younger brothers was named after their grandfather, James MacGregor. James MacGregor Patterson was born in Wellington on 26th April 1900. At first he went into teaching before taking Theological studies in the Presbyterian Theological Hall in New Zealand (1929-1930), and then New College, Edinburgh. After an assistantship briefly in an Edinburgh Parish, James was ordained to the charge of Teviot in Roxburgh, of the Central Otago Presbytery on 14th April 1932. He subsequently, and briefly, served several other charges up to 1940 after which he went around doing stated supply in various places. He was unmarried and died on 4th September 1974 at Brooklyn, Wellington. Besides Grace and James, Catherine had two other daughters (Agnes and May), and two other sons (David and William), all of whom became teachers. An M.A. graduate from the University of New Zealand, Catherine had herself been a teacher. She passed away in Wellington on 20th December 1958.

James' and Grace's two youngest daughters were Margaret ('Maggie') and Charlotte ('Cha'). Margaret, who was born in Edinburgh on 10th October 1872, married a Mr David McGill, and died in 1944. Charlotte Eliza was born in Edinburgh on 3rd February 1875 and married the Rev. Robert Wood, above twenty years her senior, on 5th February 1907. Robert Wood, born on 22nd June 1853, had started life as a minister in Scotland and had come to New Zealand in 1878 as assistant in the First Church, Dunedin. At the time of his marriage to Charlotte MacGregor he was Organising Secretary and Agent for the Otago Sustentation Fund, but in 1909 he took a charge at Waikare in the Wairarapa Presbytery. He resigned this on 13th April 1913 and subsequently did Church Extension work in the Wellington District, at Island Bay and Seatoun. Robert finally retired on 23rd June 1918. He died, 11th August 1931, in Wellington, aged 78. Charlotte and he had three daughters and a son. The eldest two of the three daughters married Presbyterian ministers. Charlotte died on 28th January 1966 at the age of 90. She was the last surviving child of James and Grace MacGregor.

15

LATTER END

In the book of Psalms we read: "Mark the blameless man, and observe the upright; for the future of that man is peace" (37:37). That is a wonderful Epitaph for anyone to have. James MacGregor was an "upright man." He believed in the inspiration and authority of the Word of God and sought to apply it in his life and ministry – and in the bringing up of his many children. He had sorrows, and he had inconsistencies. But in the end he was faithful to Christ. He believed in the distinctive tenets of Calvinism. He held strongly to the doctrine of divine sovereignty and particularism of saving grace. In some ways he was the last of the great 19th Century Free Church theologians on the conservative side. Every man, however, has his time. James MacGregor's time on this earth would draw to a close toward the end of 1894 when the Lord would call him to rest from his labours.

His end in this life came with suddenness on a Monday morning in his manse at Oamaru on 8th October 1894. He had been ailing for some time and lately had been confined to the house with some form of rheumatism or arthritis. On the previous Saturday (6th) he was out for a little and seemed a bit better. At about 5 o'clock that night, however, he had some sort of seizure. The Doctor (Harry Archibald de Lautour) was called. Everything possible was done to make him comfortable and he rallied a little on the Sabbath. However, there would be no recovery and on the Monday morning at around 9 o'clock he passed from this life to his heavenly reward. He was sixty-four (or sixty-five) years of age and left a widow, Grace, a son and six daughters, besides a grieving congregation.

It is an irony that just a few months before his own passing he wrote some lines of verse on hearing of the resignation of a former acquaintance from the ministry in Scotland. The words seem to have a poignant application to himself:

> The seventy years gone from us like a dream,
> The ocean wide now crossed, the harbour near,
> The many-mansioned home is ours, we trust,
> With Father, Saviour Son, and brethren dear.
> An evening song remains – "Of sinners chief,
> For entrance wide through grace, I wait in firm belief."[1]

The funeral of James MacGregor took place on Wednesday, 10th October. The scene is well described by the *Oamaru Mail:* "A large number of the many friends of the late Dr. Macgregor were present at the funeral service conducted in Columba Church yesterday. The Church was full to overflowing. Addresses were delivered to the family and friends at the Manse, commencing at 2 o'clock, by the Revs. W[illiam] Wright (Otepopo)[2] and [William] Gillies (Timaru)

---

[1] "On Reading Dr. W. C. Smith's Letter of Resignation." *The British Weekly*, No. 401, Vol. XVI, Thursday, July 5, 1894, 166. *Walter Chalmers Smith* (1824-1908) was the minister of the Free High Church in Edinburgh (1862-1894). He was of a liberalising tendency and in earlier days James MacGregor had crossed swords with him, especially over the question of the perpetuity and application of the moral law.

[2] The Rev. William Wright (1849-1930) was successor to James MacGregor at Columba Church, which he served from 1895 to 1914.

and at 2.30 service was held in Columba Church, where the reverend gentleman's remains had been taken. The service was conducted by the Revs A. B. Todd[3] and [John] Kilpatrick (Warepa), the latter taking as the subject of his remarks "For we know that if our earthly house of this tabernacle were dissolved, we have a building of God, an house not made with hands, eternal in the Heavens.[4] For if we believe that Jesus died and rose again, even so them also which sleep in Jesus will God bring with him."[5] The solemn cortege then left the Church, proceeding to the cemetery, where the schoolchildren lined the path leading to the grave. The Rev. J[ohn] Steven (Moderator of the Church) read the service, and prayer was offered by Professor [Andrew] Harper, of Melbourne. The Moderator of the Presbytery (the Rev. P[eter] S[cott] Hay) was the only member of the Oamaru Presbytery who was not present, and he was too far away in the interior to be informed of the sorrowful bereavement that had befallen the community. Several southern ministers arrived by the express train from Dunedin to pay their last act of respect to their departed friend, and the local ministers of all denominations also attended. At a meeting of the Oamaru Presbytery held yesterday evening, the Rev. J[ohn] Steven was formally appointed interim Moderator in the vacancy in Columba Church, and it was arranged that the Rev. R[obert] [Rose]

---

[3] The Rev. Alexander Bruce Todd (1821-1903) had been a student with MacGregor at New College, Edinburgh. He immigrated to New Zealand in 1859. He was the minister in St Paul's Presbyterian Church, Oamaru, from 1869 until 1895. The closing years of his life were spent in Dunedin.
[4] 2 Corinthians 5:1.
[5] 1 Thessalonians 4:14.

M[cKay] Sutherland should conduct funeral services in Columba Church next Sunday."[6]

James MacGregor's mortal remains were laid to rest in the cemetery at Oamaru in a plot over which a memorial stone was later erected by congregational and public subscription. The gravestone was made by Messrs William Robin and Son, Paisley, and shipped out to New Zealand. It is of grey granite and stands 9ft 3in in height. The inscription reads[7]:

ERECTED

BY THE CONGREGATION AND FRIENDS

IN MEMORY OF

JAMES MACGREGOR D.D.

FIRST MINISTER OF

COLUMBA CHURCH, OAMARU

DIED OCTOBER 8TH, 1894

AGED 64 YEARS

---

[6] *Oamaru Mail*, Thursday, October 11, 1894.
[7] *North Otago Times*, Vol. XXXVI, Issue 8414, 25 February, 1896. The inscription gives MacGregor's age as 64 at his passing. From birth records it appears he may have been 65. See pages 16 and 17 above.

Stone erected in memory of James MacGregor in the
Oamaru Cemetery

James's widow, Grace, subsequently moved to Dunedin. She
survived her husband by twelve years, passing away on 15th
February, 1907.[8]

In his personal library James MacGregor left around 3000
volumes. This was subsequently sold by the family for £375,

---

[8] *Otago Daily Times*, Issue 13829, 16 February 1907, 8.

including pamphlets, periodicals (and shelving!), to the Library of the Presbyterian Theological College in Dunedin. Apparently, it contained "some very rare and valuable works."[9]

MacGregor's was an eventful life. There were great changes socially and theologically, in Scotland and New Zealand, but he held on to the old school Calvinism he had learned in the early Free Church days, under William Cunningham and the great Senatus at New College. He made his own distinctive contribution to theological and apologetic literature.

One Obituary notice highlighted what was so central to his life as a Christian and as a minister and pastor:

> ...sympathetic reverence for God's word was distinctive of him as teacher and as a man... 'Thy Word is Truth' was the deepest conviction of his soul – the motto of his life, and the key to his theology...and his absolute intellectual honesty, would have made him a Calvinist in theology, though Calvin, Augustine, and Paul had never lived or written...When the outer crust was pierced, he was a Highlander and a Christian to the core, devout and fervent in his feeling, and warm in his affections."[10]

---

[9] *The Christian Outlook*. No. 3, Vol. 2, February 16, 1895, 'The Week.' £375 would be worth around £38,000 at the end of 2014!
[10] *The Christian Outlook*. No. 35, Vol. 1, October 20, 1894, 431-2.

16

EPILOGUE

As we have seen, James MacGregor possessed a modest poetic gift. The following piece was included by him in a letter of 19th November, 1869, to John Stuart Blackie. In his letter MacGregor wrote: "I write you a contribution of *English* song, which I wrote long ago, as words to a Gaelic air, on 'Uaimh a Bhaird,' or, 'The Poet's Grave.'"[1] It seems an appropriate item with which to close this biography. The poignant sentiments have an almost mystical element to them and seem so apposite to MacGregor's own case:

I

We fain would know the hallowed spot
Where that true heart has found its rest.
We fain would learn the varied lot
Which from that heart such utterance pressed.
In vain the wish! Time's ruthless wave
Has worn away the minstrel's grave.

II

His place on earth no man can tell.
His very name has passed away.
The land and race he loved so well
No tribute to his worth can pay:-
Save that from kindred spirits wrung,
Which feel as he has felt and sung.

---

[1] *Blackie Papers*, MS 2629, National Library of Scotland Catalogue, Vol. II, Edinburgh, 1961.

III

Yet, though no outward trace remains
To mark his fate, his nobler part
Shall live in these immortal strains:-
Those strains which each responsive heart
Will kindling seize, and glad prolong,
Through his own dear-loved land of song.

IV

Sweet be thy sleep! Where'er thy dust
Is laid — in earth, or Ocean's cave,
Thy soul is now in peace we trust;
A nation's heart shall be thy grave.
Enough! thy spell is o'er us cast:
Thy work remains, thy toil is past.

"His last sermon," said a member of his congregation after the pastor's death, "may well serve to bring home to us the lesson of his life. The subject was 'The Gibeonites, hewers of wood and drawers of water,' the text being Joshua ix., 23. 'Who, then,' he asked, 'are the Gibeonites of today? They are those who are living for this world alone, and not realising the higher divine and spiritual life of man. Be they rich or poor, they are nothing but hewers of wood and drawers of water.'"[2]

James MacGregor is largely forgotten now. However, he served his own generation by the will of God and deserves to be remembered as an outstanding preacher, theologian and defender of the faith who always sought to be faithful to Christ. "Blessed are the dead which die in the Lord from henceforth: Yea, saith the Spirit, that they may rest from their labours; and their works do follow them" (Revelation 14:13).

---

[2] *The Christian Outlook*. No. 35, Vol. 1, October 20, 1894, 432.

17

BIBLIOGRAPHY (A):

PUBLISHED WRITINGS OF JAMES MACGREGOR[*]

1. Three Smooth Stones from the Brook, or A Brief Exhibition of The Case of Mr. James Lamont, The Case of the Free Church of Scotland, and The Case of the Church Established in Scotland.
Edinburgh: Johnstone and Hunter. 1853. 51pp.

2. Christianity versus Secularism, or Secularism is not the practical philosophy of the People. (Issued by the Christian Institute.)
Glasgow: James R. McNair. 1855. 16pp.

3. Hegel. Article in the *Encyclopaedia Britannica*, Eighth Edition.
Edinburgh: Adam and Charles Black. 1856. XI, pp281-284.

4. Jacobi. The same, XII, pp607-609.

5. A Vindication of Natural Theology: on grounds of Reason, Scripture, and Orthodoxy, with special reference to the Glasgow College Case, and the recent Publications of Professor Gibson.
Edinburgh: Andrew Elliot. 1859. 78pp.
_____The same. Second Edition, Revised.
Edinburgh: Andrew Elliot. 1859. 80pp.

6. Three Hundred Years Ago: A Historical sketch of John Knox and the First Reformation.
Edinburgh: Andrew Elliot. 1860. 64pp.

---

[*] This represents published writings of James MacGregor arranged in *chronological order*. Published *books* are indicated by UPPERCASE type. Otherwise no distinction is made between pamphlets, booklets or magazine articles, other than what is largely discernible from the descriptions given.

7. CHRISTIAN DOCTRINE: A Text-Book for Youth.
Edinburgh: Andrew Elliot. 1861. vii, 164pp.
_____The same. 12th Thousand.
Edinburgh: Andrew Elliot. 1874. viii, 168pp (with Index).

8. Theories of the Lord's Day – Dominical and Sabbatarian. Article
IV, *The British and Foreign Evangelical Review*. Vol. XII. No. XLIII.
January, 1863, pp93-116.

9. The Apostolic Commission: A Sermon on Luke xxiv. 47.
Edinburgh. [1864].

10. "Beginning at Jerusalem." Why Should the Gospel be Preached
first to the Jews? *The Family Treasury*, 1864, pp150-153.

11. The Inspiration of Scripture: Its Nature and Extent.
Theological Tract No. 1.
Edinburgh: Andrew Elliot. 1864. 36pp.

12. The Headship of Christ: with special reference to the Disruption
Church.
Edinburgh: Andrew Elliot. 1864. 32pp.

13. *Family Worship*. Series of Devotional Services by Ministers of the
Presbyterian Churches. 47th Week: Thursday, James MacGregor,
A.M.
London: 1864, pp642-644.

14. THE SABBATH QUESTION: HISTORICAL, SCRIPTURAL,
AND PRACTICAL.
Edinburgh: Duncan Grant. 1866. xii, 433pp.

15. Sabbath Blessings. Being a section from The Sabbath Question,
by the Rev. James MacGregor, Paisley. A very able and important
contribution on the Sabbath Question.
Printed in *The Christian Treasury*, 1866, pp193-194.

16. MEMORIALS OF THE LATE REV. HENRY M.
DOUGLAS. Minister of the Free Church, Kirkcaldy. Edited by
Rev. James MacGregor, Paisley.
Edinburgh: Andrew Elliot. 1867. 208pp.

17. Justification by Works. *The British and Foreign Evangelical Review.* Vol. XVI, No. LXII, October 1867, pp778-810.

18. Our Presbyterian Empire. *The Presbyterian.* No. 1, May 1, 1868, pp1-2.

19. Calvinistic Universalism. *The Presbyterian.* No. 2, June 1, 1868, pp3-4.

20. The Competency of Theological System. Lecture delivered on entering upon the duties of the chair (of Systematic Theology) in the New College, Edinburgh. 1868. 8pp.

21. Professor MacGregor on Hymns. *The Watchword.* August 2, 1869, pp210-215.

22. The Question of Principle now raised in the Free Church specially regarding the Atonement.
Edinburgh: John Maclaren. 1870. 76pp.
_____The same. Second edition. Revised.
Edinburgh: John Maclaren. 1870. 76pp.

23. Professor MacGregor's Speech: including A Reply to Criticism of His Pamphlet on the Question of Principle now raised in the Free Church specially regarding the Atonement.
Edinburgh: Duncan Grant. [1870?]. 47pp.

24. The Catholic Doctrine of the Atonement. *The British and Foreign Evangelical Review.* Vol. XX, No. LXXV, February 1871, pp110-135.

25. Dr William Cunningham. *The British and Foreign Evangelical Review.* Vol. XX, No. LXXVII, October 1871, pp752-792.

26. The Union Committee's New Proposal.
Edinburgh: John Maclaren. 1872. 16pp.

27. The Christian Doctrine of Creation – I. *The Christian Treasury,* 1872, pp265-268.

28. The Christian Doctrine of Creation – II. *The Christian Treasury,* 1872, pp349-353.

29. The Christian Doctrine of Creation – III. *The Christian Treasury,* 1872, pp397-400.

30. The Christian Doctrine of Providence – I. *The Christian Treasury*, 1872, pp444-448.

31. The Christian Doctrine of Providence – II. *The Christian Treasury*, 1872, pp495-497.

32. The Christian Doctrine of Providence – III. *The Christian Treasury*, 1872, pp505-508.

33. The Question of Church Property. With an Appendix. No. VI. Issued by the Scottish Disestablishment Association. (1874?). 8pp.

34. India Missions: Their Difficulty and Prospects, *The Family Treasury*, 1874, pp680-684.

35. Dr Charles Hodge and the Princeton School. *The British and Foreign Evangelical Review*. Vol. XXIII, No. LXXXIX, July 1874, pp456-469.

36. The Place of Man Theologically Considered. *The British and Foreign Evangelical Review*. Vol. XXIV, No. XCI, January 1875, pp113-137.

37. Steidheachadh na H-Eaglais an Stat: Gu H-Araidh a Thaobh Na Gaidhealtachd.
Dun-Eidinn: Maclaubhrainn & Macnibhinn. 1875. 15pp

38. Notes on the Disestablishment Question, Specially in Relation to the Highlands.
Edinburgh: Maclaren & Macniven. 1875. 11pp.

39. Disestablishment and the Highlands.
Edinburgh: Maclaren & Macniven. 1875. 12pp.

40. Servum Arbitrium. *The British and Foreign Evangelical Review*. Vol. XXIV, No. XCIV; October 1875, pp 621-644.

41. Age of the Pentateuch, with Special Reference to Revelation and Inspiration. *The British and Foreign Evangelical Review*. Vol. XXVI, No. C, April 1877, pp254-274.

42. On Revision of the Westminster Confession. *The British and Foreign Evangelical Review*. Vol. XXVI, No. CII, October 1877, pp692-713.

43. Church Membership of Infants: Practical Aspects. *The British and Foreign Evangelical Review.* Vol. XXVII, No. CIV, April 1878, pp301-327.

44. The Christian Doctrine of Creation. *The British and Foreign Evangelical Review.* Vol. XXVII, No. CVI, October 1878, pp. 724-751.

45. Reordination of Romish Priests, *The Catholic Presbyterian.* Vol. 1, No. XI (April), January-June 1879, p317.

46. The Transition from Philosophy to Theology. *The British and Foreign Evangelical Review.* Vol. XXVIII, No. CIX, July 1879, pp501-520. (Inaugural Lecture, delivered in the New College, Edinburgh, 6th Nov. 1878.)

47. THE EPISTLE OF PAUL TO THE CHURCHES OF GALATIA. With Introduction and Notes. (Handbooks for Bible Classes and Private Students).
Edinburgh: T. & T. Clark. 1879. 127pp.

48. Nature of the Divine Inspiration of Scripture. *The British and Foreign Evangelical Review.* Vol. XXIX, No. CXII, April 1880, pp201-219.

49. "The Apostolic Commission: A Sermon", in, *Modern Scottish Pulpit.* Sermons by Ministers of Various Denominations. Vol. II., Edinburgh: James Gemmell, 1880, pp176-190.

50. Rev. John Bruce, D.D., Free St. Andrew's, Edinburgh. In *Disruption Worthies – A Memorial of 1843.*
Edinburgh: Thomas C. Jack. 1881, pp79-86.

51. Doctrinal Position of the Cumberland Presbyterians, U.S. *The Catholic Presbyterian.* Vol. V No. XI (February), January-June, 1881, p152.

52. The Resurrection of Jesus: As a Doctrine and as a Fact. In a volume entitled, *Revealed Religion.*
No details of original publication, pp113-130.

53. Balquhidder, Rob Roy, &c. Being an address to the Gaelic Society of Dunedin.
Dunedin: "Daily Times" Office. [1882?]. 14pp

54. The Land Question: With Special Reference to New Zealand and Old Scotland.
Dunedin: J. Wilkie. 1883. 40pp.

55. Regarding Evolution. The Previous Question of Science.
Paper read at a meeting of Otago Institute, 13th October (1886?).
Dunedin: John Horsburgh. [1886?]. 20pp.

56. The Previous Question of Science regarding Evolution. *The British and Foreign Evangelical Review.* Vol. XXXV, No. CXXXVIII – October 1886, pp731-763.

57. The Day of Salvation (2 Cor. vi, 2) obscured in a recent pamphlet on "The Reign of Grace".
Wellington and Dunedin: New Zealand Bible, Tract, and Book Depot. [1888]. 72pp.

58. EXODUS, With Introduction, Commentary, Special Notes, &c.
Part I. The Redemption – Egypt.
(Handbooks for Bible Classes and Private Students).
Edinburgh: T. & T. Clark. 1889. 207pp.

59. EXODUS, With Introduction, Commentary, Special Notes, &c.
Part II. The Consecration – Sinai.
(Handbooks for Bible Classes and Private Students).
Edinburgh: T. & T. Clark. 1889. 181pp.

60. Freedom in the Truth under Shield of a Constitution of Government and of Doctrine, in accordance with the Word of God.
Wellington and Dunedin: New Zealand Bible, Tract, and Book Depot. [1889]. 72pp.

61. Blown in the Wind or Growing by the River? Presbyterians on Trial by their Principles.
Wellington and Dunedin: New Zealand Bible, Tract, and Book Society. 1890. 40pp.

62. THE APOLOGY OF THE CHRISTIAN RELIGION. Historically Regarded with Reference to Supernatural Revelation and Redemption.
Edinburgh: T. & T. Clark. 1891. 544pp.

63. Panic and the Fear of God. *The Expository Times*. 1891/92, p104. (From, *The Apology of the Christian Religion*. T. & T. Clark. 1891.)

64. Socialism and its bearings on Capital, Labour, and Poverty. *The Bibliotheca Sacra*. Vol. XLIX, Article II, January 1892, pp30-61.

65. Socialism. *The Presbyterian and Reformed Review*, Vol. III, No. 9, January 1892, pp35-63.

66. Bearings of Socialism on Morality and Religion. *The Presbyterian Quarterly*, 6.1 (January 1892), pp67-88.

67. A Political Sermon on the primary formation of a people, or New Zealand's *Index Expurgatorius*.
North Otago Bible in Schools Association. 1892. 10pp.

68. THE REVELATION AND THE RECORD. Essays on Matters of Previous Question in the Proof of Christianity.
Edinburgh: T. & T. Clark. 1893. xii, 265pp.

69. The Sacredness of Family, Guarded by Affinity as Bar to Marriage with Near of Kin. Historical exhibitions of Practical Bearings and Scriptural Grounds.
Wellington and Dunedin: New Zealand Bible, Tract, and Book Depot, 1894. 25pp.

70. STUDIES IN THE HISTORY OF CHRISTIAN APOLOGETICS. New Testament and Post Apostolic.†
Edinburgh: T. & T. Clark. 1894. ii, 370pp.

† The spine of this volume, in the only edition produced by T. & T. Clark, has *History of New Testament Apologetics*. MacGregor never did have a copy of this volume in his hands as he passed away before it was distributed.

71. As to Ritschlism. *The Christian Outlook*. No. 46, Vol. 2, December 14, 1895, p539.‡

72. The Free Offer in the Westminster Confession. *The Banner of Truth*. Number 82-83, July-August 1970, pp53-58.
[Reprinted from "Blown in the Wind or Growing by the River? Presbyterians on Trial by their Principles" (1890)].

73. James MacGregor on the Westminster Confession. *The Monthly Record of the Free Church of Scotland*, February 1971, 30-32.
[Reprinted from "Blown in the Wind or Growing by the River? Presbyterians on Trial by their Principles" (1890)].

74. Christ and the Sabbath.
London: Lord's Day Observance Society, 1971. 22pp.
[Reprinted from "The Sabbath Question" (1866)].

75. Amyraldism. *Peace and Truth*. Volume 52, May 1973, pp2-6.
[Reprinted from "The Question of Principle now raised in the Free Church specially regarding the Atonement" (1870)].

---

‡ MacGregor wrote many contributions to periodicals, magazines and papers in New Zealand. We include this item as his last contribution, published after his passing.

18

BIBLIOGRAPHY (B)

MAJOR SPEECHES OF JAMES MACGREGOR
IN THE FREE CHURCH ASSEMBLY,
1859-1880

1. *Proceedings and Debates of the General Assembly of the Free Church of Scotland.*
Held at Edinburgh, May 1859. (Edinburgh: James Nichol, 1859).
Glasgow College Case. Page 75ff. See pages 138-142:
Speech by Rev. James MacGregor, Barry.

2. *Proceedings and Debates in the General Assembly of the Free Church of Scotland.*
Held at Edinburgh, May 1863. (Edinburgh: James Nichol, 1863).
Union with United Presbyterian Church. Page 180ff. See pages 234-236:
Speech by Rev. James MacGregor, Paisley.

3. *Proceedings and Debates of the General Assembly of the Free Church of Scotland.*
Held at Edinburgh, May 1867. (Edinburgh: James Nichol, 1867).
Case of the Rev. Walter C. Smith. Page 80ff. See pages 159-164:
Speech by Rev. James MacGregor, Paisley.

4. *Proceedings and Debates of the General Assembly of the Free Church of Scotland.*
Held at Edinburgh, May 1871. (Edinburgh: J. Maclaren & Son, 1871).
The Union Question, Page 129ff. See pages 132-139:

Speech by Professor MacGregor.
Report on National Education, Page 208ff. See pages 220-221:
Speech by Professor MacGregor.

5. *Proceedings and Debates of the General Assembly of the Free Church of Scotland.*
Held at Edinburgh, May 1877. (Edinburgh: J. Maclaren & Son, 1877).
The Case of Professor Smith. Page 90ff. See page 125:
Speech by Professor MacGregor.

6. *Proceeding and Debates of the General Assembly of the Free Church of Scotland.*
Held at Edinburgh, May 1880. (Edinburgh: J. Maclaren & Son, 1880).
Disestablishment Debate. Page 123ff. See pages 135-136:
Speech by Professor MacGregor.
The Case of Professor Smith. Page 170ff. See pages 189-193:
Speech by Professor MacGregor.

19

BIBLIOGRAPHY (C)

SPECIAL STUDIES

1. Cameron, Hector, "The 'Hymns' Question and Professor MacGregor's Memorial," in *The Monthly Record of the Free Church of Scotland*, December 1968, 242-245.

2. Keddie, John W., Introductory Note to, James MacGregor, "The Free Offer in the Westminster Confession," in *The Banner of Truth*, Number 82-83, July-August 1970, 51-52.

3. Keddie, John W., "James MacGregor on the Westminster Confession," in *The Monthly Record of the Free Church of Scotland*, February 1971, 30-32.

4. Keddie, John W., "Professor MacGregor, Dr Laidlaw and the Case of William Robertson Smith," in *The Evangelical Quarterly*, Vol. XLVIII. No. 1. January-March 1976, 27-39.

5. Keddie, John W., "James MacGregor and His Significance in Relation to Scottish Theology in the Nineteenth Century," in *The Banner of Truth*, Issue 158, November 1976, 26-33.

6. Breward, Ian, "Lloyd Geering and James MacGregor: Two New Zealand Apologists," in James Veitch (Editor), *Faith in an Age of Turmoil: Essays in honour of Lloyd Geering*, London 1990, 190-202.

7. Keddie, John W., "Professor James MacGregor: Theological and Practical Writings, 1868-1881,' in *Scottish Reformation Society Historical Journal*, Volume 1, 2011, 109-127.

8. Keddie, John W., "Professor James MacGregor and the Case of William Robertson Smith," in *Scottish Reformation Society Historical Journal*, Volume 2, 2012, 197-219.

THE AUTHOR

Born in Edinburgh in 1946, John Keddie was educated in the city and trained as an Accountant after leaving School in 1965. He moved to London in 1971, and qualified as a member of the Association of Chartered Certified Accountants (1976); worked in London up to the end of 1982, including a spell as Commercial Manager of the marketing section of Dunlop Sports Company; and entered the ministry of the Free Church in Scotland in 1987, serving at Burghead (Morayshire)(1987-1996) and Bracadale (Isle of Skye)(1997-2012). In 2000 Mr Keddie adhered to the Free Church of Scotland (Continuing) and retired from his pastoral charge there in April 2012. He acted as lecturer in Church History and Church Principles in the denomination's Seminary in Inverness between 2008 and 2019.

Mr Keddie wrote the official history of the Scottish Amateur Athletics Association, published in 1982 [*Scottish Athletics*]. Subsequently he produced two biographies, one of an outstanding Scottish 19th Century minister and theologian, *George Smeaton* [Evangelical Press, 2007] and the other an acclaimed biography of Olympic Champion, Eric Liddell [*Running the Race*, Evangelical Press, 2007; 2nd Edition, 2012; 3rd Edition, 2020]. On Eric Liddell he also produced *Finish the Race* for younger people, [Christian Focus Publications, 2011]. He has also written a popular book on the singing of Bible Psalms in worship, *Sing the Lord's Song* [2nd Edition, 2003] and has written widely for sports and Christian papers and magazines.

Married to Jean (since 1971), John and Jean Keddie have 4 children and 11 grandchildren. John Keddie's brother, Gordon, is a pastor in the Reformed Presbyterian Church of North America and is the author of many popular evangelical commentaries.

Printed in Great Britain
by Amazon

33090407R00119